JACQUES DE GUÉLIS

JACQUES DE GUÉLIS
SOE'S GENIAL GIANT

His Life, His War & His Untimely End

Delphine Isaaman

UNIFORM

This edition first published by Uniform
an imprint of Unicorn Publishing Group

Unicorn Publishing Group
5 Newburgh Street
London W1F 7RG

www.unicornpublishing.org

A catalogue record for this book is available from the British Library

ISBN 978-1-911604-44-0

Printed and bound in Great Britain

Cover design Uniform Press
Typeset by Vivian@Bookscribe

Dedicated to the memory of
Jacques Vaillant de Guélis
who didn't live to tell his own story
and to all the other SOE agents
who never came home.

CONTENTS

FOREWORD

This book about Jacques Vaillant de Guélis reveals a man of immense bravery, to match his stature. Using his great leadership and organisational skill, Jacques made a significant contribution to the success of the SOE in France during World War II for which he was highly decorated.

I am delighted to be invited to write this Foreword. I have studied the members of the Special Operations Executive (SOE) French Section for thirty years. My interest began after family visits to France in the 1980s when I was intrigued by memorials which are not seen in Britain, simply because we were not occupied. These memorials are to people who died in the war after deportation to concentration camps or as hostages who were summarily shot. Consequently, I decided to learn more about the brave people of the French Resistance and it soon became very clear to me that the British were greatly involved. It is comforting to note that the French are belatedly becoming aware of the part played by the SOE in training, arming and co-ordinating sabotage and insurgency. General Eisenhower claimed that the effectiveness of the French Resistance shortened the war by nine months.

In May 1940, Winston Churchill was appointed Prime Minister, just before the evacuation of the BEF at Dunkirk. Shortly afterwards France was defeated. For the first time in British history, we could not land troops onto mainland Europe. Churchill had experienced warfare several times and realised the value of fighting the enemy from within. The SOE was formed to harass the enemy; to sabotage factories and infra-structure; and eventually to prepare for the day when we could finally invade and liberate Europe. SOE operated in all occupied countries – France being arguably the most important as it was to be the location of the landings on D-Day.

But who were the SOE agents? The main attributes were to have excellent language skills, to be resourceful, brave and dedicated. Jacques de Guélis had all these skills and he volunteered to serve his two countries with the aim of liberating France. Jacques had been attached to the British Expeditionary Force as interpreter and liaison officer and, after escaping via Dunkirk, he returned to France and eventually managed to escape over the Pyrenees. Soon after his arrival back in England in March 1941, he was recruited by the newly-formed French Section of SOE and became one of its first agents. Despite having first-hand experience of the severe consequences of operating behind enemy lines, he volunteered for his first mission to France the following August and was parachuted back into his father's country with another agent, near Montluçon.

During his time in France, Jacques made many different contacts and gained priceless information about life under enemy control. A month later he was the first SOE agent to be picked up from occupied France by Lysander and he returned safely. For a while, Jacques worked in the London HQ of F-Section, sharing his up-to-date knowledge with trainees. Then in 1943, Jacques served at SOE's base in Algiers and was involved with the French in the liberation of Corsica. His third mission in July 1944 took him to the centre of France as co-leader of an inter-allied mission of seven men sent to liaise with Maquis groups.

Jacques is listed on my website as one of the 425 agents of SOE French Section that operated in France during World War II. His story is just one of many that could and perhaps should be told.

Delphine Isaaman has thoroughly researched her subject using interviews with family members and with some of the major war-time figures in SOE. She has consulted all the available books, records and reports. Delphine has gone the 'extra mile' to exhaust her sources.

This biography remembers a special man with a proud and exciting war record who sadly had his life cut short by a dubious car accident soon after peace was established in Europe.

David M Harrison
Lytham St Anne's, UK
March 2018
www.soe-french.co.uk

'Marie-Louise n'aime pas les mandarines'

Message to reception groups at Chadebec announcing the parachute landings
of the SAS andJedburghs on the night of 10/11 June 1944 at La Fontfreyde

'Du petit tondu au grand frise'

BBC message to Tilleul with intructions

Preface

Because of his untimely death, Jacques de Guélis left us no word about his wartime exploits. By all accounts he was a man admired and liked by many, although, as M. R. D. Foot has noted, he was suspect in SOE because of his interest in politics. He was known to be right wing and yet… he was sent to France in 1941, where many of his contacts were committed socialists.

Then he was sent to Algeria in 1942–43, where his skills as a negotiator in a chaotic situation were valued by both SOE and the French. He was an admirer of General Henri Giraud and this regard was reciprocated. He went into Corsica with another admirer, General Henry Martin. After Corsica was liberated, his connections with these men worked against him and General de Gaulle wanted nothing more to do with him and he was sent back to London.

He does seem to have touched peoples lives: his driver in 1939–40, who kept a record of his activities and subsequently wrote a eulogy after his death; the Belgian agent he debriefed in 1945 and who later wrote a touching letter to his widow; General Chambe who promised that they would meet up again after the war; Paul Colonna d'Istria who saw him as his friend and 'camarade de guerre' and understood his antecedents.

And there were many more.

He has left the impression of an attractive and likeable man, a *bon viveur* with extraordinary charm but also a man with tact and delicacy when dealing with his fellow men. Above all he was courageous and honourable in the best traditions of France and the land of his birth.

1

FAMILY ORIGINS, CHILDHOOD AND EARLY MANHOOD (1907–39)

Precise answers to certain questions were required. To get these answers first hand, Jacques de Guélis, a genial giant of a man, descended on France.

'Secret Service, Set Europe Ablaze' by
Jerrard Tickell – *The Sunday Express*
1 May 1949, p.2

FAMILY BACKGROUND

Three miles north-east of Sancergues, in the French Department of Loir-et-Cher, is the pretty little village of Herry. Like all church property, it was seized by the state at the time of the Revolution and subsequently sold to private individuals. The lands at Herry were acquired by a Baron Charles-Emmanuel Micoud d'Umons (1753–1817), a *Baron de l'Empire*[1] and a Prefect of the Department of *l'Ourthe*, in Belgium, from 1806 till the fall of the Empire. But many of the surviving noble families who had stayed in France were ruined and obliged to rebuild their fortunes. Thus it was that during the first quarter of the nineteenth century, a certain Jacques Vaillant de Guélis (1774–1886), desperately in need of employment after the recent upheavals, came to Herry and took up a post on the new Baron's estates. But as his surname already existed in the area, it is quite possible that he had been born and brought up not far away. As time went by, Jacques was in a position to buy a parcel of land from the Baron, possibly before

1840, and this estate, called Villatte, remains in the hands of the same family today. Villatte has changed little in the intervening years. Just outside Herry the farmland is flat, and at Villatte maize is grown and sheep are reared. The present owner keeps magnificent hounds for hunting and the locals poach fish from the lake just as they have done for centuries. The house itself is built of mellow stone, has hardly changed since the 1930s, and has an unpretentious and comfortable interior.

Villatte, the de Guélis family home in Herry, France

The Vaillant de Guélis family is a very ancient one indeed, and unlike other noble families who have a coronet in their coat-of-arms, the de Guélis arms has merely a knight's helmet. This is unusual and pre-dates the coat-of-arms of more recently ennobled families. According to the present owner of Villatte, the Vaillant de Guélis family is mentioned in the archives of the Château de Seganges, near Avernes in the Allier, and originated as local seigneurs in Metz-le-Comte, in the Nivernais, as early as the twelfth century. Certainly, the name de Guéllis, with two l's, had appeared by the fourteenth century and had become de Guélis by the early fifteenth century. So it is possible that around this time a de Guélis performed so well in battle that he was awarded the right to add Vaillant – 'the valiant' – to his family name. A de Guélis was Bishop of Orléans in the sixteenth century. By the seventeenth century, members of the Vaillant de Guélis family are to be found in the Department of Cher, at Herry, Menetrol-sous-Sancerre, Aubigny-sur-Nère and Grimonville. Also, a de Guélis who was born in Orléans, moved to Canada and became Superior of the Jesuit Order in Montreal in 1709.

Raoul Vaillant de Guélis (1872–1916), the father of the subject of this biography, was born at Villatte, Herry, and being a member of this noble family, expected to inherit the estate or perhaps a share of it according to French inheritance laws, like his father, Théodule Vaillant de Guélis (1840–1925), before him. But as Raoul, despite his noble origins, had to earn his living the hard way, he came to South Wales some time before World War I and joined Sam Powell's firm of coal exporters that exported to the west coast of France. Interestingly, coal merchant, John Yeo- Thomas, father of Forest Yeo- Thomas – SOE's *White Rabbit* – moved his family in the other direction, to Dieppe. It was in Cardiff that Raoul de Guélis met his future wife, Marie Stéphanie Barbier[2] (1875–1958), the eldest daughter of Professor Paul Eugène Emile Barbier (1846–1921) who, after starting his career in school-teaching, had moved to Cardiff in 1883 to become a Lecturer in French Language and Literature at the newly established University College, Cardiff.[3]

The Barbier family originated in the villages of the valley of the River Doubs in the Franche Comté, a strongly Protestant region of eastern France, to the east of Besançon, that forms a natural frontier with the western end of Switzerland. Paul Eugène's father, the widowed Georges Barbier (1819–92), Jacques' maternal great-grandfather, had, together with three children from his first marriage, come to London in 1861 to work as a Protestant missionary among the French poor in Soho. On 2 December 1864, he married his second wife – Jeanne Marie Chapuis (b.1831), in the Swiss Church, Endell Street, London – and the couple had six more daughters three of whom survived to adulthood: Mathilde (b.1865), Georgine (1867–1953) and Marie Louise Charlotte Blanche (1873–1927), who in 1896 married Charles George Vallencey (1866–1927). The family eventually settled in

Raoul de Guélis in uniform

Professor Paul E. E. Barbier, grandfather of Jacques de Guélis

10, Charlotte St, London, where the second Mme Barbier ran a guest house for French-speaking Swiss Protestant girls who were seeking posts as governesses or language teachers. It was here that Paul Eugène Barbier met the Swiss/French Euphémie Marie Bornet (1848–1923) when she was en route to Sweden to a post with the Swedish Countess of Hamilton. They married in Aubonne, Switzerland, on 13 September 1872.[4] After some years teaching French at Felsted School in Essex, Paul Barbier was dismissed for absenting himself without leave (Craze, 1955, pp.182–3), he then taught French at Manchester Grammar School from where he was recruited in 1883, aged thirty-five, by the new University College of South Wales and Monmouthshire. (*See note 3*)

Into this strongly Protestant family – part Lutheran and part Calvinist – came Raoul Vaillant de Guélis, a Catholic. He and Marie Stéphanie married at St Peter's Church, Cardiff, on 10 August 1904 after a wait of several years, partly

Marie de Guélis

Monsieur & Madame Théodule
Vaillant de Guélis ont l'honneur de vous
faire part du mariage de Monsieur Raoul
Vaillant de Guélis, leur fils, avec
Mademoiselle Marie Barbier

Villatte, par Herry (Cher)
le 10 Août 1904.

Wedding invitation

due to the objections of her father and then because of a law suit in France, with a civil ceremony at the French Consulate the previous day. Their first child, Jacques Théodule Paul Marie Vaillant de Guélis, was born at 3, Richmond Terrace (now 3 Museum Place), Cardiff on 6 April 1907 and their second, Jacqueline, in 1912. Raoul always hoped that his wife would allow the two children to be brought up as Catholics, but sadly, he was not destined to see his children grow up, and on his death-bed in the Argonne (19 April 1916), serving as a Brigadier (Corporal) in the French Army, he expressed his hopes for their upbringing to the Chaplain who attended him.[6] In Cardiff, Jacques and Jacqueline grew up alongside two orphaned cousins – Delphine (1913–1996) and Georges ('Val') Barbier (1917–1992). Their father, Georges Charles Barbier (1876–1921), was Marie's slightly younger brother and he also worked in the coal industry; he was reputed to be able to hold a piece of coal in his hand and tell the mine from which it came. So, when both he and his wife Annie ('Nan') (1886–1918) died young, the widowed Marie de Guélis took on their children and brought them up as her own. Tragically, Jacqueline was killed in a road accident in Cardiff in 1934.

Marie de Guélis had four surviving brothers and four sisters; two babies,

3, Richmond Terrace, Cardiff

Announcement of Jacques' birth

Ernest, (1879–1880) and Eugène Edmond (b. and d. 1890), had died in infancy. Jacques grew up within a large, close family, all of whom spoke French. His maternal grandfather, Professor Paul Barbier senior, was an ebullient character who was thought by some to be the model for the Paul Barbier who appears in the novel *The History of David Grieve* (1892) by Mrs Humphrey Ward (1851–1920). He was certainly well-known in the Cardiff area, and immortalised by Howard Spring (1889-1965) in Heaven Lies about Us (1939), the first part of his autobiographical trilogy.[7] Paul had a drink problem which may explain, in part, the impecuniousness of his family. (*His father had a property in Montaure, Normandy, understood to have been bought with his second wife's dowry. This was known locally as the Chalet Barbier and was occupied by some of the daughters from the second marriage, possibly into the 1940s. The author visited it while on holiday when it was owned by Parisians as a holiday home. They said that when they bought it, they found the attic full of whisky bottles!*)

Holidays were often spent at Villatte, where Barbier aunts and uncles were frequent visitors, and while there Marie de Guélis would attend mass in Herry Church. There were shooting parties and other family gatherings there.

There were other cousins, two of whom were killed as a result of World War II. Lieutenant Paul Eric Aver Duncan, RNVR (MiD) (b.1914), was killed in action on 8 November 1942, aged twenty-eight, while serving aboard the sloop HMS *Walney* during Operation Reservist, the Allied landings at Oran during the invasion of North Africa).[8] Major Raoul Paul Cuthbert Hepburn, RASC (*MiD*) (b.1916), lost his life in Germany, aged twenty-nine, on 17 November 1945, as a result of a wire that was stretched across the road in front of his vehicle.[9] The cousins got on well, and having been brought up together, Jacques and Val Barbier were particularly good friends despite the ten-year age gap between them. Jacques' aunt, Isabelle Barbier, personal assistant to Dame Maud McCarthy in World War I and later a Dominican nun, wrote on 12 March 1946, 'Jacques, Eric and Val were brothers – but brothers loving, understanding and helping each other – happy together.'

Jacques 1908

Jacques held by his aunt Isabelle Barbier

Back in Cardiff, Marie and her family received visits from their Barbier cousins who lived in Leeds. Her elder brother, Paul Émile A. Barbier (1873–1947), had followed in his father's footsteps by becoming an Assistant Lecturer in French at the Yorkshire College in 1899 (i.e. before it became the University of Leeds in 1904), and occupying the Chair of French there from 1903/04 to 1938. So when he was called up to serve in the French Army in August 1914, his wife, Cécile Ernestine Barbier née Delaloye (1875–1971), whom he had married in 1906, and her five children came to stay for a while in Cardiff.[10] Sadly, the youngest child, Euphémie, would die on 20 November of that year, while her father was in the village of Erquinghem-Lys. The circumstances of her death, coupled with Cécile's fragile mental health, led to estrangement with her husband's family which was never resolved. Cécile's two eldest children, Paul Georges, known as Pépol and Marie, remained in Cardiff for a while and Pépol was able to play with Jacquot, as Jacques was known in the family, and attend the same school.

College school play – Jacques seated right with his cousin Paul behind

During the post-war years, Professor Barbier *fils*, with four remaining children of his own, was very popular with his many nephews and nieces. They wrote regularly to thank him for birthday and Christmas presents and to tell him about their academic successes and even their love life. (*The author also received Christmas and birthday presents regularly from her grandfather.*) Paul's mother and his sister Marie, who had difficulty making ends meet, frequently appealed to him for loans, as did his periodically impecunious nephews and nieces, Jacques among them. And even while the latter was serving as a liaison officer at the beginning of the World War II, he still wrote to his Uncle Paul requesting a loan.

With his sister and nurse

Fancy Dress

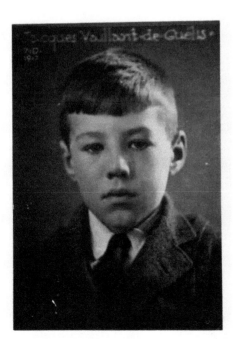

Above: Jacques in sunhat

Left: Portrait 1917

SCHOOL AND UNIVERSITY

After attending Llandaff Cathedral School, Jacques became a pupil at Wrekin College, at Wellington, Shropshire (founded in 1880), from 1921 to 1925. He was a member of Saxon House and became its Head of House from Easter 1923 until July 1925, and also a member of the first rugby XV, though not its Captain. In 1925 the Old Wrekinian Association was able to offer for the first time a bursary or exhibition to a boy who was leaving to go to university. Jacques was the first recipient of that award, having been given an Exhibition worth £40 per annum by Magdalen College, Oxford, to read for a degree in PPE (Philosophy, Politics and Economics) under the acerbic tutelage of T. D. ('Harry') Weldon (1896–1958), Fellow in Philosphy 1923–58), who later became 'Bomber' Harris' chief wartime intelligence officer. But Magdalen was one of

The 1ˢᵗ XV of the 1924-25 season.

Wrekin College 1st 15 – Jacques 2nd right (C.A.)

Wrekin College, Jacques head of Saxon House 1925. Seated right of the House Master
(C.A.)

the most expensive Oxford colleges. Douglas Dodds-Parker (1909–2006), who came up to Magdalen as a Commoner to study History a year behind Jacques (1927–30) and who would later become his superior officer in SOE,[11] received £350 per annum from his father. But by scrimping, renting a modest room, and economising on such consumables as fuel and food, it was possible to get by on as little as £140 per annum (Brockliss, 2008, pp. 464–7). Nevertheless, Jacques' family must have had to rally round with money to quite a considerable extent, given the paucity of funds in his immediate family.

A young woman called Elsie McLachlan was a particular friend of Jacques, and in spite of a visit to Canada in the summer of 1925 to meet her parents, nothing came of it.

Jacques matriculated at Magdalen in autumn 1926 and left in 1929 with a third-class degree. The College Archives have nothing to say about his activities while he was there, but given his class of degree, it is probable that, as was the case with

Canadian visit

many of the post-war generation of undergraduates, work was low down in his order of priorities. He was a member of the Magdalen College Dramatic Society and had parts in their December 1926 production, as did J(ohn) Betjeman. Moreover, the Magdalen tutorial authorities, being in the closing years of the presidency of the once brilliant, ambitious and formidable Sir Thomas Herbert Warren (1853–1930; Fellow of Magdalen 1877–1930; President of Magdalen 1885–1928; Vice-Chancellor of Oxford University 1906–10 [see Brockliss, 2008, *passim*, but especially pp. 402–17), do not seem to have been inclined to do much about the situation since there is no record of Jacques receiving any kind of reprimand or warning.

Among the friends he made at Oxford, was Patricia Hardy, a French-speaking undergraduate who graduated from Somerville College in 1928 with a second-class degree in French and Spanish and at whose wedding in Pau in south-west France he would be best man (1930), resplendent in his French cavalry uniform. Coincidentally, in 1993, some sixty-six years later, Patricia's son, Duncan Stuart, became SOE advisor to the FCO and helped researchers like myself. While

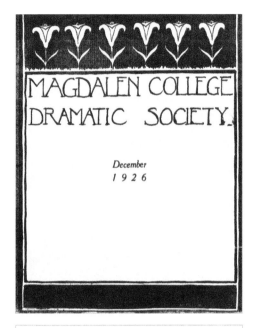

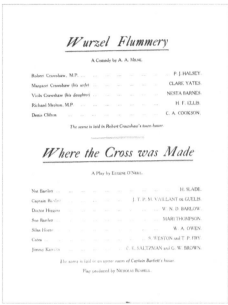

Magdalen College Dramatic Society 1926

Jacques was at Magdalen, his world would, on the whole, have been populated by well-connected people like Douglas Dodds-Parker – although two of his cousins were also up at Oxford: Paul G. R. Barbier (who got a 2nd class in Honours

Wedding of Patricia Hardy at Pau, 1930.
Jacques in military uniform (D.S1)

Moderations (Classics) at Queen's in 1929) and his sister Marie Barbier, at St. Hugh's. Their father was Professor Paul E. A. Barbier – Paul G. R. Barbier, his eldest son, had won several scholarships. In her (unpublished) memoirs Marie Barbier commented that her cousin Jacques wasn't working enough, that there were too many distractions. Also that he had great charm and attracted a host of friends. The cousins met frequently and there were noisy parties held by Jacques and his room-mate. Marie Barbier also remembered having lunch at Magdalen with her cousin and friends to meet a graduate called Pat Hardy.

Although Jacques was born in Britain, he had dual nationality and, following the family tradition spent two years doing military service in France, like four of his Barbier uncles before him. As he was very tall – 6ft 3in – he went into the cavalry. He began his two years as a trooper on 29 October 1929 and was promoted to *Brigadier* (Corporal) on 14 March 1930, then *Brigadier chef* (Corporal-of-Horse, i.e. Sergeant) on 15 April 1930. In February 1931, his service completed, he was promoted *Maréchal des logis* (Warrant Officer) in the Reserve and as such, was required to take part in manoeuvres from 12 to 31 March 1934. While in the Army, he was able to visit his Uncle Edmond Barbier in the rue Antoine Boucher, Paris, and also his paternal grandmother, widow of Theodule de Guélis, who had died in 1925, at Villatte. After the 1914–18 war, Edmond Barbier had remained in Paris with the Claims Commission and was living there with his Danish wife Karen Gottfredson (an agent for Royal Copenhagen Porcelain) and their four children. The family would eventually return to England and settle in Surrey in 1933.

In a letter to his brother, Paul, of 23 February 1931, Edmond wrote that he had

Military Service

seen a lot of his nephew during the past eighteen months and would miss him when he left for England.

After his time in the Army, Jacques opted for a career in advertising. He became an advertising manager with Philco (Great Britain) 1931–32, an advertising manager with Addressograph (France) 1932–35, and an advertising consultant 1935–39. (Hutchins and Sheppard, 2004, p. 84). By 1931 he was living in Chelsea when in Britain and staying with his Uncle Edmond during his trips to Paris. But by 1933, so Marie de Guélis reported, Villatte, now in a very neglected state, as it had been empty for two years, belonged to him and his sister Jacqueline. Letters suggest that, apparently, there were family discussions on what to do about the property: sell it, or accept help from a relative? It seems they soldiered on, perhaps with family help, of which I have no record, as many old manor houses do, and the property was finally passed on to another member of the family by Jacques' widow, Beryl, where it remains to this day.

Jacques on horseback at Provins during military service

On 26 February 1938 Jacques married Beryl Richardson (1904–78) in Kensington and lived in West London, and in 1939 he joined John Haddon and Co Ltd. This wedding must have been a very quiet affair as there appear to be no surviving photographs of the young couple together although a wedding invitation survives. The wedding took place in London so maybe few of the Cardiff family could attend.

Jacques was inordinately proud of his French ancestry, and when he visited Villatte, he received invitations from all the other landed families in the district. One imagines that he was also popular with their daughters: how disappointing it must have been for them that he chose to marry in England! Like the present owner of Villatte, he enjoyed hunting and shooting, having served in a cavalry regiment during his military service, he would have been able to ride round the estate on horseback. There were also relations on his father's side to visit with whom he could discuss their royalist hopes and dreams.

But it was 1939, and the outbreak of war would change things forever. Jacques was obliged to re-join his regiment in France and his dual nationality was about to play a significant part in the coming years.

Jacques with moustache

MRS. HARRY CHRISTOPHER RICHARDSON
HAS THE HONOUR OF ANNOUNCING
THE MARRIAGE OF HER DAUGHTER

BERYL

TO

MONSIEUR JACQUES VAILLANT DE GUÉLIS

WHICH TOOK PLACE AT ST. AUGUSTINE'S,
QUEEN'S GATE, ON SATURDAY THE TWENTY-
SIXTH OF FEBRUARY, NINETEEN HUNDRED
AND THIRTY-EIGHT.

34, SUMNER PLACE,
LONDON, S.W 7

1938 – Jacques and Beryl's wedding invitation

Beryl de Guélis

Shooting party at Villatte – Jacques second from left

FOOTNOTES

[1] The Nobility of the Empire was created by the Emperor Napoleon in order to establish a stable elite after the French Revolution by amalgamating the old nobility with the revolutionary bourgeoisie. In 1804, the title of Prince was bestowed on members of the imperial family: Dukes followed in 1806 and Comtes, Barons and Chevaliers (Knights) in 1808. Many of these titles were given to military men, over a thousand Barons were created, and some descendants of this new nobility still exist.

[2] Marie Stéphanie Barbier was Professor Barbier's eldest daughter and second of his children.

[3] The second son of 'Pasteur' Georges Barbier, Paul was educated in Paris, but abandoned his original intention of becoming a minister of religion to become a school-teacher. He began his professional life teaching French for a year or two at Felsted School, Essex, and he then taught at Manchester Grammar School before moving to Cardiff (1883), where he ultimately became Professor of French. Paul was active in the promotion of Franco-Welsh relations and the Entente Cordiale (8 April 1904) – for which he received a personal letter of thanks from King Edward VII. He published several school editions of French classics and was made an *Officier de l'Académie* and an *Officier de l'Instruction Publique*; see [Anon.], 'Professor Paul Barbier [obituary]', *The Times*, no. 42,842 (4 October 1921), p. 13, col. C. His son, Paul Émile A. Barbier (1874–1947), followed in his father's footsteps and became Professor of French Language and Literature, and Romance Philology at the University of Leeds in 1903. The University of Edinburgh awarded him an Honorary LL.D. on the occasion of his retirement; see [Anon.], 'Edinburgh', *The Times*, no. 48,347 (3 July 1939), p. 8, col. D.

[4] The Hamiltons are a distinguished Swedish family descended from two brothers, sons of Captain J Hamilton of Co. Fermanagh, Ireland and were mercenaries in the Thirty Years War. In Sweden, as in many other countries, all sons inherit a title. Countess Hamilton was the second wife and widow of Jacob Essen (1794–1864). They married in 1861 and had two children, the eldest, Stéphanie, being Euphémie's charge. Information from the Duke of Hamilton's estate.

[5] According to Census records, Paul Eugène was already teaching at Felsted in 1871; MGS has no record of the dates or the nature of his employment.

[6] Raoul de Guélis died on 19 April 1916, of pneumonia. H. Cougel, the military chaplain for Ambulance 2/10, Secteur 72, wrote to his mother on 26 April 1916 . Another letter was written by a comrade, Jules Follin (to either his mother or his wife) – of the 11ᵉ Régiment d'Artillerie à pied, 69e Batterie, Secteur Postal 7.; He was buried at the military cemetery at Ste. Menehould and re-interred at Herry in 1921. (Family letters seen but present location unknown.) Raoul left nearly £3,580 in his will – *c.* £108,000 in 2005. Invested at 4%, this capital sum would have brought in £143 p.a. and a careful family would have been able to live reasonably comfortably on such a sum.

[7] Howard Spring (1889–1965), a very successful journalist and author, came from Cardiff. Mrs Ward issued a denial and an apology to Paul Barbier, senior.

[8] Eric was the son of James Hugh Duncan, brother of Annie Duncan, James married Marie's youngest sister Euphémie (1887–1953). The Walney was originally built in 1930 as a Banff-class coastguard cutter for the US Navy (USS *Sebago*) and handed over to the Royal Navy in 1941 as

part of the lease-lend agreement. It was originally used to escort convoys, but on 8 November 1941 it and a sister ship were ordered to smash their way into Oran Harbour and land troops despite point-blank fire from French warships and shore defences. Both ships were sunk and the majority of the 241 soldiers and 81 crew being carried by the Walney were killed. The only officer to survive was the Walney's CO, Captain Frederick Thornton Peters, DSO, DSC & Bar, RCN, who was awarded the VC for his part in the action, only to die just three days later when his flying boat crashed off Portsmouth. See [Anon.], 'Royal Navy', *The Times*, no. 49,421 (17 December 1942), p. 7, col. E. Eric Duncan was last heard on deck appealing to the French not to fire as they were on the same side. Also a letter of 2 December, 1942 to Eric's mother from Jocelyn Betthall, Captain RN. (Family papers).

[9] Letter of 11 December 1945 to Paul E. A. Barbier, fils, from Jenny (Jennet) Hepburn, Raoul's widow. Raoul was the only son of Charles J. Hepburn (d. 1926), who married Marie's younger sister Uline Julie Barbier (1884–1964) in 1915. At the time of Raoul's death, his wife and small daughter Alexandra were living in Argyll, Scotland. He is buried in grave VI.F.7 in Cologne Southern Cemetery.

[10] Paul Georges (1908–74), Marie Cécile D. (1909–2003), Cécile E. (1910–1994), Albert Francis A. (1912–71) and Euphémie (1913–14).

[11] Magdalen College Archive (where the Dodds-Parker papers are now held).

2

THE PHONEY WAR, FLIGHT AND CAPTURE AND EVASION (1939–41)

C'est la gauche qui a exploité la Resistance,
mais c'est la droite qui l'a crée.

François Grossouvre (personal adviser to François Mitterand)
Quotation taken from *Le Combat de Paul Dungler* by Jean Eschbach

THE PHONEY WAR (1939–40):
(LA DROLE DE GUERRE)

Jacques was recalled to the colours on 4 September 1939 and, because of his height, had to have a special uniform made for him. His mother and her sister Euphémie had been at Villatte since July 1939, and when war broke out they were there still waiting for the money from rents so that they could return to Britain. Val Barbier, Jacques' cousin, had made himself useful there on the estate during the summer and returned to Britain with Beryl, Jacques' wife, in September. In August, Jacques' uncle, Professor Paul Barbier from Leeds visited Villatte with his friends the Milnes, but remembering his experiences in World War I, he curtailed his visit to France as the likelihood of hostilities increased, leaving his friends to continue their travels alone. When Marie and Euphémie were eventually able to travel, it took them four days to reach Cardiff, where they arrived on about 15 October. By that time they were aware that Jacques had become a liaison officer with the *Mission Française de Liaison* (the French military mission to the British Expeditionary Force [BEF]), and that he was being posted to Laval, in Normandy. But, first, he had gone to Orléans from where his father's cousin, Raymond Vaillant de Guélis, could send his mother news of him.[1]

Jacques in specially made uniform due to his height, 1939 (WM)

On 2 October 1939, Jacques was attached to the 234th Field Company, Royal Engineers, a territorial unit that was known as the 'Tyneside Sappers' and was part of CRE II Corps.[2] According to Sir Brooks Richards (1918–2002), who would get to know him well later in the war because of their SOE activities, he also acted as the personal interpreter of General Lord Gort, VC (1886–1946), the GOC of the BEF, and R. P. Reynolds, Jacques' driver, recorded that he was at times involved in HQ activities. But as his work as a liaison officer with a field unit mirrored that of two of his Barbier uncles – Paul and Edmond – during World War I, he wrote to his Uncle Paul from the field to tell him so and ask about their life as interpreters (letter to Paul Barbier, 4 November 1941). Both uncles have left diaries and letters describing their duties – from which it transpires that while both men acted as interpreters when required, their most frequent chore was finding billets for the men. (Diaries held by the author.) But while Paul had to arrange the equipping of a laundry and organising Christmas dinner for the mess in the village of Erquinghem-Lys, Edmond was frequently involved in public health issues, sometimes in nearby Nieppe, so the brothers contrived to meet quite frequently. And in 1914–15, Paul Barbier was to acquire lasting fame in the village of Erquinghem-Lys, a mile to the south-west of Armentières. Somehow, amid the mayhem of war, he managed to compile a dictionary of the local *patois* which survived and was published after his death, making him a local hero who is

234 Field Company, Royal Engineers Company (TNA)

remembered with gratitude to this day.[3] Family tradition has it that if Paul heard an unusual word while he was interpreting for an officer, he would embark on a long discussion as to the origins of the word and forget what he was doing!

The 234th Field Company arrived at Laval, south of Cherbourg, at 05.30 hours on 1 October 1939 and then marched to St Ouën des Toits, about seven miles to the north-west, where it settled into billets in schools and farms before setting off to fulfil their first military duty in France as Royal Engineers: the construction of latrines for HQ in Laval.[4] So this was how Jacques made his first contribution to the outcome of World War II![5]

On the following day, the Company received orders to move in three stages by road to the Arras area. Second Lieutenant Smith, who was attached to II Corps supply column, and Jacques left by road for Evreux, the first staging area, which was over to the east. On 6 October, an advance party that included Jacques and Smith, went ahead again to the second staging area at Molliens (au Bois) via Gournay (en Bray) Marseille, La Chapelle and Poix (de Picardie). Finally, on 8 October, they went to 234 Concentration Area at the village of Villers Brûlin, about 15 miles west-north-west of Arras, passing through Doullens, Lucheux, Grand Rullercourt, Avesnes (le Comte) and Aubigny (en Artois). By the end of the month, the Company was in Libercourt, 20 miles to the east of Arras, and experiencing difficulties due to the 'boggy nature of the soil'. Part of Jacques' work was to obtain information on the subject from local people and appears to have spent some considerable time researching the subject of mud and its effects during the winter and early spring of 1939/40.

November was wet, which, as the older members of the Company would remember only too well, made all outside work, especially digging, very difficult. The appalling weather was decisive in persuading Hitler to postpone his plans for a *Blitzkrieg* drive through France not once, but on several occasions, until it became too late in the year for such an attack to begin before spring 1940. So although this delay allowed the BEF to grow from 158,000 men on 11 October 1939 to 316,000 men on 13 March 1940, it also meant that thousands of men were stagnating in a strange country with all the attendant dangers of boredom and demoralisation. Thus, ways of keeping the troops busy, occupied and entertained had to be created. All of which explains why, on Sunday 26 November, while the Company was still at Libercourt, Jacques conducted his first French class in the canteen following a request from the men, and the Company's official War Diary (see note 4) records that there would be two short lessons a week. Before moving on to Bovigny, off the north-south Béthune-Arras road near Souchez, the Company received a letter from the Deputy Mayor of Libercourt, thanking them for their irreproachable behaviour during their stay and including among the named officers 'Monsieur Vaillant de Guélis, your very devoted collaborator'.

The German Army smashed into France and the Low Countries on 10 May, and advanced so rapidly, even through neutral Belgium, that on 26 May 1940, it was decided to withdraw the BEF to the Dunkirk perimeter. Engineer units were put to work preparing bridges and causeways over flooded areas for demolition and allocated sectors of the front which they were to prepare for defence and hold if attacked. A corridor had, of course, to be left open through Belgium and Northern France for as long as possible to allow troops to get to Dunkirk for evacuation. As the War Diary mentions, Jacques only rarely and, like so many War Diaries at this time, was lost for the crucial month of May 1940, we learn most about his activities for the period September 1939 to mid-June 1940 from a brief diary which his driver, R. P. Reynolds, in direct contravention of Standing Orders, kept of his movements:[6]

September 24–29, 1939 – Attached to the Company for liaison duties near Laval. Moved to Villers Brûlin, off the Arras – St Pol road to organise the billeting of the Company.

October, 1939 – Arranged the Company move to Librecourt, between Carvin and Seclin. Was very involved in II Corps HQ activity.

November, 1939 – Arranged the Company move to Bovigny, off theArras – Béthune road near Souchez. The Deputy Mayor of Bovigny would be most helpful with information.

February, 1940 – On leave in England.[7]

March – On a course with a French unit for 10 or 14 days at, possibly, St Pol, but might be St Lô.

April, Arranged the Company move to a village about 10 miles west of Amiens for a 2–3 weeks bridging training exercise.

May 10 [the date when the Germans invaded France and the Low Countries (DI)] – returned to Bovigny.

May 12 – Moved to Alost in Belgium

May 13–June 1 – Worked in the marshalling yards at Jet, a suburb of Brussels. Moved into the square in front of the Hotel de Ville [Town Hall], and from there demolished five bridges over the (Albert??) Canal running through the city.

Moved back to Lille and set up HQ in the Madeleine section of the city.

Moved back into Belgium and saw action near Poperinghe and Menin.

Moved back to a bridge about 10–20 miles inland from Furnes, built a pontoon bridge and prepared it and an iron permanent bridge for demolition. The Company was cut off and as the firing order was 'On contact with the enemy', the bridge was 36 hours late in being blown.

He (Jacques) stayed with the demolition party whilst the Company escaped through a gap that had been left for them.

Reynolds added that, 'The above information given is from my personal experience as I was his driver with the 234 Field Company, RE, and I was equally involved, except for his leave and the course'.

DEFEAT AND FIRST FLIGHT TO ENGLAND (MAY–JUNE 1940):

To replace the official Company War Diary for May 1940, someone typed up a retrospective record of the last days leading up to Dunkirk. As the Company spent much of its time in Belgium reconnoitring bridges for possible demolition, Second Lieutenant Fowke got himself arrested by the Belgians and had to be cleared by Jacques.[8] On 15 May, 234 Company moved from Welle to Berchem St Agathe on the western outskirts of Brussels, where it received orders to reconnoitre six bridges over the Willebroek Canal with a view to their destruction

– which answers Reynolds' query about the canal's name (see page 40). During its subsequent retreat southwards to La Madeleine, near Lille, the Company encountered refugees jamming the roads and had to find their way using grass tracks. By now things were becoming desperate. 234 Company had orders to destroy Lille's telephone exchange and find a way to 'dope' petrol stores, as fire was prohibited in case it spread to Lille itself.

By 28 May, the Company's No. 1 Section with Second Lieutenants Welch and Fowke had retired north-westwards through Belgium from Lille via Nieuwkerke (Neuve Église), Poperinge and Proven (a mile beyond that). The route was, as the diary states, *choc à bloc*. Meanwhile, No. 2 and 3 Sections set off in the same general direction from Wulverghem but lost contact with each other on roads that were equally packed with transport. Indeed, the situation was so bad that Jacques and Major Clothier, who had stayed behind to oversee the departure of all three Sections, did not succeed in rejoining the Company before its embarkation.On 29 May, two sections with Second Lieutenants Fowke and Agar[9] moved to Furnes (Veurne), a mile away from the Belgian coast and five miles north-east of the French frontier, and were instructed to help another RE unit prepare bridges over the Bergues-Furnes Canal for demolition.

On 30 May, the Company was reunited and moved south-westwards to La Panne (De Panne), a little town near the Belgian coast behind Furnes, where it was instructed to start work on a pier for embarkation that was to be built between high and low water. This was done by driving abandoned lorries onto the sands, parking them side by side, and lashing them together, thus forming a causeway into the sea over which it was possible to retreat. At daybreak on 31 May, after waiting overnight on the beach, the Company started to embark via the pier using rowboats. But where was Jacques? Reynolds said later that they had lost touch at Dunkirk, which is not surprising, but that he did manage to escape [perhaps] on a small sailing vessel.[10]

His dual nationality and the fact that he was attached to a British unit, may have allowed Jacques to stay a few days longer in England than most of the *c.*140,000 French troops who had been evacuated from Dunkirk, since, before returning to France, he was able to see his wife and mother. Many French troops who landed in England were sent, initially, to Tidworth, on Salisbury Plain, and from there many were repatriated within forty-eight hours in order to continue the fight against the Germans.

In a letter dated 5 June 1940, Jacques' mother writes to his cousin Val saying that Jacques had rung up on Thursday evening [that would have been 30 May if correct] asking her to come to Tidworth, to let Beryl know and not to be disappointed if they found him gone. Beryl, having got her message late, jumped on a train at Paddington then a taxi and did the rounds of all the barracks with difficulty in the black-out, and finally found him at 2 am. They spent two and a half days with him. Apparently he wasn't allowed to go out of his hotel but had to be escorted and called for. 'We met him at a place near Tidworth called Ludgershall. He was fit but a little stunned.' She went on to say that when he reached the agreed meeting place on the beach, the others had gone. He left the car and when he returned the men with him had been killed. He collected some more men and waded to a small boat while being machine-gunned all the time. A man on either side of him was killed in the boat. He came back on the HMS *Icarus*[11] which had accounted for five German ships outside Narvik. She went on – 'very few of his company were left alive'. He said they were shot in the back by Belgian civilians, maybe 5th Columnists. He didn't sleep for a week and fought for a fortnight. He had seen to blowing up bridges in Brussels and they blew up all the bridges as they came away. He said he would never forget Belgium. Marie de Guélis also added that La Charité, the nearest town to Villatte had been bombed.

Some were sent back even more rapidly – in one case going from Dover to Plymouth and embarking on the return journey to France in approximately twenty-four hours. It is estimated that only fifty per cent of those French troops who were repatriated to France actually saw action before the Franco-German Armistice, which was signed near Compiègne on 22 June 1940 in the self-same railway carriage as the Armistice in 1918 and came into force on 25 June (see Loosely, 2006).[12]

RETURN TO FRANCE, CAPTURE AND EVASION (JUNE 1940–MARCH 1941):
Still in the French Army – his French military record states that he was demobilised on 6 August 1940 – Jacques returned to France via Southampton and Cherbourg on 11/12 June,[13] probably as a liaison officer once more. Whereas Sir Brooks

Richards thought that he was with a British unit, Sir Douglas Dodds-Parker believed that he was with the partially trained 1st Canadian Division. In either case, he was taking part in Operation Ariel, under the command of General Sir Alan Brooke (see note 3), the evacuation of the *c.* 200,000 Allied personnel who had been left in France after the end of the Dunkirk evacuation (2 June). These troops were either still fighting in central northern France or were situated well south of the River Somme. Either way, they were untouched by the rapid German advance across northern France which reached Abbeville on 20 May and ended on 12 June with the surrender of the badly mauled 51st (Highland) Division and some French units under General Erwin Rommel (1891–1944) at the little fishing port of St Valéry-en-Caux.

Once OPERATION DYNAMO – the Dunkirk evacuation – had been completed on 2 June 1940, Churchill decided to send the 52nd (Lowland) Division (TA) and the 1st Canadian Division to France for two reasons, and he communicated that decision to the Supreme War Council at the Château de Muguet, near Breteau, on 11/12 June. He wanted to first boost the morale of the French, and second, to assist in the evacuation of the *c.* 200,000 British and Allied troops mentioned above. Elements of 52nd Division – the 156th and 157th (Infantry) Brigades – landed at Brest and Cherbourg on 8 and 12 June respectively and moved to the area around Evreux, in Normandy. Part of the Canadian Division landed at Brest during the same night (11/12 June) that Jacques landed at Cherbourg. But when Brooke arrived at midnight on 12/13 June, he soon realised that the military situation was hopeless and on the following day persuaded Churchill by phone that withdrawal was necessary. So before they had had a chance to fight, the Lowland Scottish, part of a contingent of *c.* 30,000 troops that included the British 1st Armoured Division, withdrew from Cherbourg between 15 and 17 June, and the Canadians, part of a contingent of *c.* 21,500 troops, re-embarked for England from St Malo on 16/17 June.

But Jacques was not among these units and it is probable that if he was taken prisoner by the Germans it might have been not long after his return to France, when the French Army finally surrendered on 25 June 1940. But M. R. D. Foot states that, '…he had been taken prisoner and had made an adventurous escape to England with André Simon the younger'. Unfortunately, M. R. D. Foot was not permitted to give his sources. One author says that he was captured in Boulogne.[14] Where Jacques was taken prisoner and when remains a mystery. His personal file states that he and André Simon were taken prisoner and attempted three or four unsuccessful escapes. One may assume that this came from Jacques himself. His cousin Val Barbier, who also later became an SOE officer, stated that he retreated with the French Army and was demobbed in Toulouse, down in the south; whilst his personal file, tells us that he retreated to Marseilles.[15] As these unsuccessful escape attempts seem to have been before being demobilised on 6 August 1940, it is worth dwelling for a while on what this may mean. First of all, as it was the Germans' practice to assemble long columns of prisoners and march them eastwards towards long-term internment in Germany, Jacques may never actually have been incarcerated but simply escaped from loosely guarded captivity or a column on the march. Indeed, as members of the Armed Forces were advised to attempt escape as soon after capture as possible, such escapes did occur,[16] and two French women are on record for pulling out a captive from a column of prisoners and giving him civilian clothes.[17] Then again, although Jacques' French military file gives 6 August as the date of his demobilisation, the dates on his telegrams to his wife and mother make it quite clear that he was at liberty in unoccupied Southern France in July, i.e. well before that official date. The only mention of his captivity is in M. R. D. Foot's book and we must assume he was correct. In fact there is no mention of captivity by the Germans in any of the numerous family letters. On 31 July 1940, Marie de Guélis wrote to her brother expressing her concern for her son as he would have neither money nor civilian clothes and on 24 July his wife Beryl received a telegram that had been sent on 4 July saying that he was at Thuir. (A commune in the Pyrénées-orientales, 13 km from Perpignan.) Marie de Guélis received a closely written note from Jacques from Thuir. The first part dated 20 July 1940 states that he is well and still in the Army. On the 25th he is concerned for the family, that Cardiff may be bombed and that Villatte is in the Occupied Zone. He has written to people there with no response but is worried that Villatte is damaged as there has been fighting nearby. He had also written to Solange (de Neuville at the Château de Combas, a relative). On the 31st he had heard from his mother. Then Jacques must have turned back because another telegram to his wife that is mentioned, is dated December 1940, and came from the Hotel Pharo in Marseilles' harbour district: '*Bon courage – t'embrasse ainsi que Maman de tout coeur. J de G.*'

Beryl de Guélis had replied to Thuir and her letter had been forwarded (mentioned in a letter from Marie de Guélis). André Simon's wife believed that the two refugees had stayed at some stage in the safe house of Dr George Rodocanachi (*1875 or 76–1944 †[KZ-Buchenwald]*) at 21, rue Roux de Brignoles, Marseilles.[18] If she was correct, then it must have been on this early occasion since on another later occasion her husband hid in the house of Louis Nouveau, (*Capitaines par Milliers by Louis Nouveau –1958 p.23*). He arrived there on 7 July, 1942). Moreover, during Jacques' time on the run, weeks and months passed with no news from him at all. Given Jacques' connections, he may have been given Rodocanachi's name at the end of 1940 when he was in Marseilles, because in that year Dr Rodocanachi was already treating evaders from the British Sailor's Mission, directed by the Rev Donald Caskie (d.1983).

On 13 September 1940, Val Barbier wrote to his uncle, Professor Paul Barbier, that nothing had been heard for two months and, after the war in a letter of 7 September 1945, Jacques' mother wrote to her brother, the same Paul Barbier, referring to 1940–41, when it had taken her son four months just to escape from Marseilles and that Jacques' wife Beryl had been advised by General de Gaulle's office in London not to visit the family home, Villatte, in the village of Herry or the town of La Charité sur Loire, as the Germans were very near. Family sources say that Villatte was never occupied by the Germans. Some family members left Paris during the 'Exodus' and found refuge with relatives at the Château de Combas, south of Limoges and one uncle took refuge in St Malo.

Could it be that one or more of the three 'escape attempts' were not from the Germans in the North, but from Southern France and over the Pyrenees into Spain. Perhaps M. R. D. Foot's use of 'adventurous' gives a clue. In fact Marie de Guélis mentioned in a letter to Val Barbier that Jacques had tried to get out of France four times but crucially he made no attempt to leave until he was demobilised. He was, she said, Demobilisation Officer until the end of July and his first attempt was made last August. She also added that he was changed and looked much older, 'which you will understand when he tells you everything'. Val Barbier, in his 1984 letter, maintained that Jacques, Simon and another companion first tried to get away by sea: they embarked at night, but their boat sank and they had to start all over again. Perhaps the weather in the Pyrenees had been against them, or guides failed to turn up. Downed airmen and SOE agents might carry silk maps to help them escape. These did not rustle or crackle and could be easily concealed about one's person. There are several in the family which show the Pyrenees and the ways through them which may have belonged to Jacques – these date from 1943 – the 43 series had double-sided maps in colour.

But by November 1940, an organisation had been established in Marseilles to help escaped British personnel to get out of both the occupied and the unoccupied zones of France and into Spain via the Pyrenees. Val Barbier believed that Jacques had been guided over the mountains by a smuggler, and it is probable that Peter Churchill and an Alsatian evader were guided over those mountains by just such a person. In Churchill's personal file, Jacques tells him to contact someone called Tché, who he knew and whose brother has boats, but this fell through as the brother had been arrested.

In the above mentioned *Des Capitaines par Milliers* both Virginia Hall and Pat O'Leary, alias the Belgian doctor Albert-Marie Guérisse (1811–1989), stayed there with Louis Nouveau. (It is worth mentioning that all the names recorded by Louis Nouveau were inscribed in Volume 44 of the *Complete Works of Voltaire*.)

There is, unfortunately, no way of knowing if Peter Churchill's proposed guide was the same man, but the Pyrenees must have been a magnet for smugglers for centuries, not to mention religious fugitives like the Cathars who were seeking refuge from the Inquisition on the far side of the Pyrenees. One of the many escape lines later became known as the *Pat Line* after Pat O'Leary (see above)[19] and it used the two safe houses that we have already come across. Guides took groups of men, in the main downed airmen, over the Pyrenees for a price, usually several thousand francs. Hazards included being abandoned by the guides en route, bad weather and capture by the Spanish authorities on the other side. And, of course, there was always the danger of betrayal – and the *Pat Line* had a traitor in its midst. Sergeant Harold Cole (1906–1945), alias Paul Cole, a petty crook, fraudster and deserter who was finally shot dead by the French police in a Paris flat in 1945, brought groups of escapees south through France and eventually betrayed a large number of people, including a priest, who had been helping escapers and evaders by printing false documents (see *Des Capitaines par Milliers*, pp.444–450: letters from prison by the Abbé Carpentier, the priest who was betrayed by Paul Cole; see also *Saturday at MI9* by Airey Neave, pp. 307–311).

But did Jacques stay put in the South between July 1940 and the date when he crossed the Pyrenees in the winter of 1940/41? Or did he move about and visit relatives and friends? At this early stage of the war he would have been perfectly at home and, with care, able to circulate in either zone. But if this was the case, then no record exists of his activities in autumn 1940, except snatches of information like those we have gleaned already and, here is a curious thing, found on a French extreme right-wing website. It says that in the Indre at the end of 1940, several members of the banned, extreme right-wing *Solidarité Française* decided to rejoin a small movement, soon to be called *COMBAT*. The head of the group was a Colonel Armand Plat, an Army man of the old school, who was in his sixties, tall and distinguished, and with a shock of white hair. He was joined by two former *Camelots du Roi* (members of a royalist youth organisation) who are named as Jacques Renouvin (1905–1944), a Parisian lawyer and militant royalist who joined the Resistance and died in KZ-Mauthausen (Austria) in 1944, and Jacques Vaillant de Guélis, *'futur agent du SOE britannique'*.[20]

Similarly, in his published MA thesis of 1975, Michel Jouanneau talks of the rebirth of the above organisation, which he believed took place at Châteauroux in late 1940/early 1941. One of the three men who met to discuss the idea was Louis Chevalier (1911–2001), a teacher and a distant cousin of de Gaulle, and the others were Paul Bellier (d. 1964), a tradesman and Professor Charles Sadron (1902–1993) (a Professor of Physics at the University of Strasbourg, who was originally from Châteauroux). A second meeting took place on the following day at the home of a retired Colonel, i.e. Armand Plat, who had been President of the Indre section of *Solidarité Française*. Here, six named persons attended, plus two 'other persons', and they elected Plat President, with Paul Bellier as his Deputy. They also agreed to form a local Resistance movement and set out at once to recruit members in Châteauroux. As, nearly a year later, Jacques would admit to Jean-Pierre Bloch that he had been a *Camelot du roi* but had broken with *Solidarité Française*, he could well have been in the Indre towards the end of 1940 and it would have been quite in character for him to have associated himself with a Resistance movement that leaned to the right.

Capture on the other side of the Pyrenees meant internment, and in early 1941, Jacques was caught and put into a concentration camp just outside of the city of Miranda del Ebro, in northern central Spain, not that far from Burgos. (In Jacques' personal file at Kew, but any record of his experience or any report appears to have been 'weeded' or destroyed.) Although André Simon is not mentioned here, Val Barbier, in his account of Jacques' activities maintains that Simon and another person escaped with Jacques or at least made one attempt by sea which failed. Certainly they did not arrive back in the UK at the same time. (Enquiries to the Spanish authorities failed to find any record of their names at the prison.)

'Miranda' had been in use quite recently, during the Spanish Civil War, and conditions there, relative to their German counterparts, were just about tolerable for evaders en route to Britain who were in reasonable health and could expect rapid release. There was, however, overcrowding, a serious lack of water and the food was inadequate which led to scabies and other ailments.[21] Sir Samuel Hoare (1880–1959), who was British Ambassador to Spain from 1940 to 1944 and whose main task was persuading General Franco to keep Spain out of the war, was kept busy arranging the release and repatriation of British prisoners, sixty-five of whom were in Spanish concentration camps on 18 January 1941.[22] Some time in early 1941, the British Embassy arranged the release and repatriation of Jacques [and André Simon perhaps at a later date].[23] He arrived back in Britain on the Strathmore via Spain and Gibraltar on 13 March 1941, followed by André Simon on 17 March.[24] Jacques called at Cardiff on 19 March to collect some clothes. Another letter from Marie de Guélis to Val says it was sickening about Jacques' furniture which he had cared for and which had been hers when she married. This must have been at Villatte where some things had been stolen.

FOOTNOTES

[1] Letter from Marie de Guélis to her brother Paul, 12 September 1939 (Barbier family papers).

[2] During the 'phoney war' of 1939–40, II Corps, one of the first three Corps to constitute the BEF, was fortunate enough to be commanded by one of Britain's most brilliant generals: Lieutenant-General Alan Francis Brooke (1883–1963), later GOC Home Forces May 1940– December 1941 and CIGS (therefore Churchill's senior military adviser) from December 1941 to 1946. For six days in May/June 1940, he was replaced by Lieutenant-General Bernard Law Montgomery (1887–1976). Brooke had been brought up in south-west France, knew Patricia Hardy's family (see Chapter 1), and probably met de Guélis and André Simon (1907–1978); code-name Diastique; see note 16) – another liaison officer, who would escape over the Pyrenees to England with de Guélis in 1940/41 (see note 5) – while they were under his command since it was allegedly he who later recommended them for work in the SOE. General Sir Brian Horrocks (1895–1985), who commanded the 2nd Battalion, the Middlesex Regiment, in Brooke's II Corps during the phoney war and was himself singled out for rapid promotion by Montgomery, would later say in his autobiography, *A Full Life* (1960), that the more he studied the French campaign, the clearer it became to him 'that the man who really saved the BEF was our own corps commander Lieutenant-General A. F. Brooke' (pp. 80–81).

[3] *The Great War Magazine*, Issue 9, September, 2003. *Words at War* by Delphine Isaaman, pp. 5–8 Lexique du Patois d'Erquinghem-Lys (Nord), by Paul Barbier, Ancien Professeur à l'Université de Leeds. Musée de Picardie, Amiens, 1980. A seat with a plaque, outside the Town Hall commemorates him as well as a display in the village museum.

[4] See the Company War Diary, WO167/985 (National Archives), kept by the Coy CO, Major Clothier.

[5] The world of liaison officers is rather a poorly defined one. There must have been quite a number of them collected from various nationalities and several names crop up in this story. In the second report that de Guélis made after his 1941 mission to France, he refers to another liaison officer who had been attached to II Corps: a 'Capitaine Merrick' (Captain Georges Meric appears several times – in Lord Brooke's reports and diaries [2001, p. 86], in Hugh Sebag-Montefiore's book on Dunkirk [2007, pp. 404–5 and 630n]. He reported angry scenes between French and English troops waiting to embark and in Peter Churchill's cover story, as a contact whose name was given to him by de Guélis where he was to remind Meric of the pleasant suppers they had together at the little restaurant on the seafront near the Pharo (hotel in Marseille) [Peter Churchill's personal file NO. HS9/ 314–315]) – and also Erik Wesberge (mentioned by de Guélis in his first report on his return from his 1941 mission 'Façade'). Philippe Liewer (1911–1948), alias Major Geoffrey Staunton (code-names Hamlet and Clément) – a French journalist, later recruited by de Guélis – Gérard Henri Morel (1910–60) (code name Paulot), and Forest Yeo-Thomas (1902–1964) among many others who also served as liaison officers. It is also probable that this is how he came across the explosives expert Edward 'Teddy' Bisset (1915–1944†), who was in the BEF's Intelligence Corps in Belgium and France since de Guélis, according to Jon Wilson (a relative of Bisset's who is researching his career), was to be an usher at his wedding on 31 October 1942 (as was Peter Harratt who took part in the Dieppe raid in 1942). Both Bisset

and de Guélis came out via Dunkirk and along with André Simon (see below) were, all three on Mission Tilleul in 1944. It was in France, too, that de Guélis met André Simon (see note 4), with whom he would subsequently escape over the Pyrenees in early 1941. Simon, whose father was also called André Simon (1877–1970) and who became a well-known doyen of the wine trade, was French, whereas his mother was English. André junior first joined the French Army as an ordinary *poilu* and subsequently became a liaison officer. But a note in his SOE file (HS9/1362/2) that was written by the SOE agent Bob Maloubier (1923–2015) (field name Clothaire; operational name Portier/Porter, recruited for the SOE by de Guélis at the end of 1942, after the assassination, on 24 December, of the Admiral of the Fleet Jean-François Darlan (1881–1942), the supreme commander of the Vichy French armed forces), tells us that unlike de Guélis, who spoke a most sophisticated French, Simon had a terrible French accent.

[6] The account is contained in a typescript in the Barbier Family Archive. Its origins have not been traced. Like so many others, the writer appears to have held de Guélis in high esteem.

[7] See the letter from Marie de Guélis to Val Barbier of 31 January 1940 (Barbier Family Archive): 'Jacques went back this morning by the 9.25 from Victoria. He hated going and we couldn't bear to see him go. […] You should have seen the size of the cake Mrs Richardson had made for Jacques. The baker wouldn't charge for making it as it was for a man going back to the front.'

[8] Second Lieutenant Wilmot Stewart Hanbury Fowke was still serving with 234 Field Coy when he died on active service in northern Scotland on 18 February 1941, aged 25, presumably in an accident.

[9] Second Lieutenants Welch and Agar and Major Clothier appear to have survived the war.

[10] In a letter from Val Barbier, written in 1984, describing de Guélis' activities to French relatives. Surprisingly his account was not entirely accurate which demonstrates how discreet de Guélis was even with such a close relative.

[11] HMS *Icarus*, 28 May 1940 diverted to Dunkirk. 29 May two trips from Dunkirk, carried 1,142 troops to Dover, 31 May two more trips. It looks as if de Guélis embarked on 29 May, judging by the dates his mother gives.

[12] See Loosely (2006).

[13] HS9/630/10 Jacques de Guélis – personal file, The National Archives, Kew. His cousin Val Barbier placed his demobilisation in Toulouse, in the above-mentioned letter of 1984 to the French family outlining his activities.

[14] Paul Gaujac, *Special Forces in the Invasion of France*, 1999, p. 250. No source given. M. R. D. Foot SOE in France p. 170 no source given. In 1944 while planning Mission Tilleul, de Guélis confirmed the fact that he and Simon had escaped over the Pyrenees together. GR 28 P 3 58 SHD Vincennes.

[15] Peter Churchill (1909–72) (personal file at Kew HS9/314-315) records contacting a M. 'Deprez' in Marseilles after de Guélis' return to England. He had, apparently, been one of Deprez' liaison officers and served with him at Rennes and Caen before the collapse of the French Army in 1940. Their last meal together had been a bouillabaisse at Le Restaurant Basso, 5, Quai des Belges, Marseilles, where they had discussed ways of getting through the Pyrenees. 'Deprez' was glad to hear that Jacques had arrived home safely (Churchill, 1952, *Of Their Own Choice*, pp. 134–135).

[16] M. R. D. Foot – *SOE in France*, 1966 p.170. Foot and Langley – *MI9* – Escape and Evasion 1939–45 p. 59 (paperback edition).

[17] *Conscript Heroes* by Peter Scott Janes, 2004, p. 89. For more information on escapees and safe houses see *Safe Houses are Dangerous* by Helen Long, 1985 and *MI9* by M. R. D. Foot and J. M. Langley, 1979.

[18] *Of their Own Choice*, p.139. For detailed information on Dr Rodocanachi and his activities on the escape line, Google Christopher A. Long, Dr George Rodocanachi (1875–1944†). The doctor's house in Rue Roux de Brignoles no longer exists but there is a Boulevard named after him.

[19] Google 'Conscript Heroes Pat Line' for more information.

[20] Pascallerre.hautefort.com/extreme-droite (this site appears to have been removed).

[21] Peter Janes, 2004 *Conscript Heroes*, pp. 181–186, has left us with a picture of conditions in the camp in September 1941, when about 30 British evaders (out of 2,000 inmates) were there.

[22] Later in the year the British Embassy was housing 22 escaped prisoners, some of whom had typhus, typhoid and diptheria. Hoare later estimated that between 1940 and 1944, the Embassy helped more than 30,000 escapees and evaders. See Hoare, *Ambassador on Special Mission* 1946, pp. 231 and 238.

[23] We do not know the exact date because the files in the National Archives relating to de Guélis have been destroyed or 'weeded', even though the FO Index 1941 recording his release, repatriation and financial assistance survives. (K3206/766/299 & K4635/766/299 appear to be no longer extant and FO371/269/B was 'weeded'). In general, de Guélis' file contains far less information than those of most of his immediate colleagues. Why?

[24] SOE personal files Jacques de Guélis (HS9/630/10) and André Simon (HS9/1362/2).

3

'SETTING EUROPE ABLAZE': THE BEGINNINGS OF SOE (1941)

A large, burly man, cheerful companion,
honourable and reliable, charming and
courageous, with politics far to the right
of Louis XIV.

Douglas Dodds-Parker, cited in Hutchins
and Sheppard, 2004, p. 85.

THE INTRODUCTION TO F SECTION (MARCH–MAY 1941)

Jacques immediately reported to the War Office, where, according to Sir Brooks Richards, his arrival caused quite a stir. It was not just that he was 'urbane, well-educated and with considerable charm', he was one of the first educated Englishmen to observe conditions and attitudes in Vichy France. So, realising that Jacques was exactly the kind of person who was needed in the newly formed F Section of his particular brain-child, the clandestine and independent secret service known as the Special Operations Executive (22 July 1940–15 January 1946), it seems to have been common knowledge that Churchill invited him for a lengthy personal interview. It is worth noting here that SOE was in existence before General de Gaulle's appeal to the French in June; Jacques' moment had come.[1] He was recruited by Major Lewis Evelyn Gielgud, (1894–1953), the elder brother of Val Gielgud (1900–81), the broadcaster, and Sir John Gielgud, OM, CH (1904–2000), the actor, who had been a Classical Demy (Scholar – i.e Half a Full Fellow) at Magdalen College, Oxford (1912–14). He was then interviewed – again perhaps by the same Major Gielgud – at 6, Arlington Street on 26 March

1941, and joined F Section on 15 April 1941 barely a month after his return to Britain.[2]

Set Europe Ablaze!

Initially, Jacques was given the rank of Lieutenant in the British Army, a Regular Army Emergency Commission on the General List, and was to be 'specially employed, without pay and allowances from Army Funds'. He was assigned a personal number: 184312. He worked at first in a general advisory capacity and then as a conducting (or escorting) officer for the so-called 'Inter-services Research Bureau' at SOE's HQ at 64, Baker Street, and on 19 June, the day of his promotion to Captain, Harry Nathan Sporborg (1905–85), private secretary to the 3rd Lord Selborne (1817–1971) (who had replaced Sir Hugh Dalton at the Ministry of Economic Warfare), had appointed him F Section's briefing officer. His duties included acting as conducting officer which was very important because he would accompany would-be agents to training schools all over the country where training officers, many of whom were experts in a particular field, such as Gavin Maxwell of *Ring of Bright Water* fame, W. E. Fairburn (co-inventor of the Fairburn-Sykes knife for hand-to-hand combat) and actor Peter Folis who specialised in disguises, (see Colonna d'Istria on disguises) who instructed them in the various arcane techniques they might need. The conducting officer stayed with any given student cohort throughout their course of training in order to be able to assess the participant's suitability for work in the field. Their role also involved accompanying agents to their airfield when they left on a mission. Conducting officers would also brief their agents on their missions – usually at Orchard Court, Portman Square, near the HQ of F Section at 64, Baker Street, where great pains were taken to avoid agents bumping into one another, being ably ushered in by the discreet doorman Park; they would escort agents on departure and meet them again on their return. According to the late Francis Cammaerts (1916–2006)[3], agents were not encouraged to make friends with each other. But it would have been strange if friendships had not been forged: Jean le Harivel (1918–2006) recalled having a meal in Soho with Jacques and Bob Maloubier remembered visiting his flat in London.[4] There were parties, and Jacques had his own party piece. (He played a saw with a violin bow!)

Echoes of Jacques' own experiences can be detected in Peter Churchill's personal file at Kew (HS9/314–315) and in his books. Jacques was involved in his briefing and helped to construct his 'history' as 'Oliver' for his 1942 mission. In this, Churchill was sent to Laval before becoming an interpreter. Jacques as we know from family letters, had also been sent to Laval. This military fiction may owe much to Jacques' own experience.

As to his orders for the mission, another Jacques recruit appears – Dr Levy in Antibes. Then Churchill was to go to Captain Meric in Marseille, although in *Of Their Own Choice*, he appears to have become 'Deprez'. Jacques was stationed with Meric/Deprez at Rennes and Caen. Churchill was told to remind Meric of the pleasant suppers they shared in a little restaurant called Basso's, on the seafront near the Hotel Pharo, where their last meal had been bouillabaisse and two bottles of Moselle, while discussing ways over the Pyrenees. The Pharo, of course was one of the hotels used by Jacques when planning his own escape into Spain and Churchill reported that he was well received there, as the proprietor, M. Robinot was a pal of Jacques. At the Hotel d'Angleterre, Churchill was shown Jacques' and André Simon's signatures in the hotel register! Jacques also asked to be remembered to the proprietor.

He told Churchill that if all other avenues failed with the guide Tché and his brother, he was to use Jacques' own escape route through the Pyrenees – which he described in detail.[5] When his superiors got wind of this, they were perturbed as they thought the information should be available to others.

A thread begins here which runs through this account, which is that Jacques was quite a *bon viveur*.

One of the chores at SOE HQ was writing to relatives of agents in order to reassure them that their relative was fine, and in her capacity as personal assistant to Colonel Maurice Buckmaster (1902–92) after he became Head of SOE in September 1941, Vera Atkins (1908–2000) took care of many of these, particularly the women agents.[6] Vera Atkins had come to London in 1933 and joined the WAAF before joining SOE in February 1941 at about the same time as Jacques, as a secretary. She went on to become Buckmaster's deputy and a formidable intelligence officer. At the time she was not a British subject, being Romanian but had adopted her mother's surname. She had the responsibility of overseeing the women agents and after the war made it her personal quest to discover the fates of the women agents who did not return.

Such letters of reassurance were also sometimes written by agents who happened to be in London, and Jacques, André Simon, Ian Mackenzie (b. 1910)[7] and Val Barbier were also occasionally required to write such letters.

As a conducting officer, Jacques underwent paramilitary and finishing training.[8] The paramilitary schools were situated in Invernesshire and numbered STS 21–25c; the finishing schools were located in various properties on the Beaulieu Estate and numbered STS 31–37b. Normally, agents did four weeks of basic training and two weeks of parachute training, after which those deemed suitable were sent to the more specialised training schools that were scattered around the country. George Connerade (d. 2006), later known as Georges de Guise)[9] told the author during a phone conversation of 2002, that he had trained at Manchester's Ringway airport with Jacques, for whom a special parachute had to be made because of his size.[10] So it seems likely that they attended STS 51b.

When an operation was planned at this early stage in SOE's existence, No. 1419 Flight[11] would confirm with F Section by 12.00 noon on the day of the operation that, weather permitting, it would take place that evening. This agent, or 'Joe' as he or she was colloquially known, would then be collected by car and accompanied by his or her conducting officer. The two of them would then be driven to either RAF Henlow in Bedfordshire to collect parachutes, and a W/T set for a 'George' (see p. 63) or if to be dropped by plane, probably to Tangmere. And as all agents were trained to bury their parachutes and flying clothes, even in open ground, without leaving a trace on the surface, they were also issued with an entrenching tool. But in France, which was chronically short of essentials, the parachutes were often spirited away by the local reception committee so that the precious silk and nylon could be used to make dresses and underwear for wives and girlfriends. Also in these early days, agents would then be taken either, and most probably, to RAF Stradishall, near Bury St Edmunds, or the secret airfield at Newmarket, also in Suffolk (see note 12, Ch. 2), and be flown to France in a twin-engined, medium-range Armstrong Whitworth Whitley Mk V or a four-engined, long-range Handley Page Halifax Mk II (see Clark, 1999, pp. 15–16). Either way, the agent would be given a meal and have his parachute fitted. But if an agent had not been trained in the use of parachutes or needed to be picked up from France, then, as with Jacques' exfiltration from the Châteauroux area in early September 1941, SOE used a small, manoeuvrable, but cramped, single-engined Westland Lysander Mk III, because of its very low stalling speed and ability to take off from and land in small fields. In such a case, the flight would either begin from or make a re-fuelling stop at RAF Tangmere, an operational base on the Sussex coast that was closer to France than any of the other airfields used by SOE.[12] Subject to the vagaries of English weather, flights took place on one or more of the eight moonlit nights per month, and the pilot would aim to drop the agent at midnight, when the moonlight was at its brightest. He would also be given different points for

Single-engined Westland Lysander Mk III

the drop so that he could make his final choice of drop-zone according to local conditions. Unfortunately, many missions had to be aborted, and a good number of aircraft had to return to base for several reasons without dropping its agents. A frustrating wait would then have to be endured until the next suitable night.

In his biography *Black Lysander*, John Nesbitt-Dufort describes his arrival at RAF Stradishall in early 1941 to find that out of No. 1419 Flight's aircraft there was only a single Newmarket Westland Lysander, which soon became his. He was then moved to where Newmarket Heath provided a long run for the take-off of the heavily laden Whiteleys.

He trained agents who would be going into the field in the complexities of selecting a suitable field behind enemy lines and how to lay out a flare path to guide the plane down. He familiarised them with the flight path of the plane and the position of the disembarkation and embarkation points (see p. 99 of *Black Lysander*).

Whenever possible Nesbit-Dufort liked to accompany the agents he had trained on their outward flight – mostly in Whiteleys – and by August 1941 he had made six trips as co-pilot with agents setting off on their mission. In Jacques' case, he accompanied the 'jovial giant' as he called him in a Whiteley piloted by

R. E. Austin on his first mission, 'THEORIM/VALIANT', on 6/7 August 1941, when Jacques and Georges Turck were dropped in the Châteauroux area.

Eventually No. 1419 Flight became No. 138 Squadron and it was with this unit that Nesbitt-Dufort piloted a Lysander in the Squadron's first drop and exfiltration when Jacques was picked up and Gerry Morel disembarked. Initially No. 1419 Flight was mostly worked with SIS and then with both SIS and SOE. There had been other drops by Lysander earlier in the year – Carte, Georges Bégué alias BOMBPROOF and then Pierre de Vomécourt (LUCAS) and Baron Emmanuel d'Astier de la Vigerie. Pierre de Vomécourt's brother, Philippe, had a château, Bas Soleil, near Limoges and met Jacques during his first mission. Many operations by Lysander were flown out of Tangmere which was nearer to France to economise on fuel. The Lysander did have an extra fuel tank slung underneath the fuselage.

SOE was split into country sections, with each country being allotted a letter – thus the section we are dealing with was designated the letter F for France. For political reasons, it became necessary for SOE to have two French Sections – one independent and non-political, was called F Section, whilst the other, Gaullist, was known as RF Section: Jacques, of course, belonged to the former. Under Buckmaster, F Section had its HQ in Baker Street from September 1941 onwards, whereas RF Section had its HQ in Dorset Square. When André Dewavrin (1911–98) – code name Colonel Passy – came to London in July 1941, De Gaulle appointed him head of the Free French 2nd and 3rd Bureaux (Intelligence and Service Action). The two eventually became known as BCRA (Bureau central de renseignement et d'action).

Much has been written about the bad feeling that existed between the two sections since de Gaulle was notoriously difficult to deal with because of his sensitivity and total belief in his destiny to save France. Certainly, he never forgave the British and Americans for what he saw as their condescending attitude towards him and he resented the existence of an independent French Section that was outside his control. He also objected to the fact that RF Section was totally dependent on the British for supplies, aircraft, and anything else they might need. But at the beginning of the war not all the French were behind de Gaulle – even after his appeal of June 1940 for all free Frenchmen to rally behind him. De Gaulle was not well-known at that juncture, and being a divisional commander he had only two stars, whereas General Georges Catroux (1877–1969), who came to England in 1940 to join his staff and was the C-in-C of the Free French forces from 1941–43, had five stars and so was the equivalent of a British Field Marshal. In direct contrast to de Gaulle, Catroux was known for his diplomacy and flexibility. However, within the chaos of 1940 France, de Gaulle emerged as someone with a positive vision and clear sense of direction that other French leaders lacked. But he neither forgot nor forgave, and this would have significant consequences in the future, both for Jacques and for others.

Jacques rapidly became a valued member of F Section and his abilities and charm soon earned him many admirers. His discretion must have been extraordinary, especially for a man of his size, as it is very difficult to pick up any trace of him during his time at Baker Street. His family may have known more than they admitted to, but they also knew they had to keep quiet lest they put his life – and that of others – at risk.[13] During this early period he briefed many agents at Orchard Court prior to their departure for France.

THE FIRST DROP AND AFTER (MAY–JULY 1941)

The first SOE missions landed in the Indre. This was not an especially important department, but it was in the centre of France and on the edge of the unoccupied zone (i.e. Vichy France). Topographically, the area was ideal for landings by light aircraft or parachute drops as it consisted of large areas of empty countryside. But another reason for choosing the Indre was the presence there of Max Hymans (1900–61) – *field name FREDERICK/FRÉDÉRIC* – the Socialist Deputy for Valençay (1928–40) and future President of Air France (1948–61) who, because of his position, had many contacts – both in the area and beyond.[14] On 10 July 1940, Hymans had voted in favour of Marshal Pétain, but he soon regretted this as a grave error of judgement and set about trying to contact the French Resistance in London. After some false starts, he managed to find someone who would send out messages via the British Consulate in Barcelona. Then, with the help of contacts in the French Ministries of Food and Commerce, he succeeded in sending out daily reports on press censorship, the German requisitioning of

Max Hymans (DH)

supplies, and the positions of German troops, but without knowing whether they would ever get through let alone be acted upon. He also emphasised that he lived only 20km from the demarcation line between occupied and unoccupied France and could therefore assist with inter-zone liaison. His messages finally got through to Thomas Cadett (1898–1982), the former BBC journalist and first head of SOE's F Section at the time of Jacques' first mission, who had lived in France before the war and knew Hymans.[15]

Hymans' persistence was rewarded on the night of 5/6 May 1941 when the English-speaking Georges Bégué (1911–93) (*alias George Robert Noble, field name GEORGES 1, operational code BOMBPROOF. After Bégué, all radio*

George Bégué – the first 'GEORGE' (PoL)

operators were nick-named Georges), the first SOE radio operator to be sent to the Occupied Zone, was parachuted in blind between Valençay and Vatan, five days before the arrival of his assigned agent, Baron Pierre de Vomécourt (1906–86) (*field names ETIENNE, LUCAS, SYLVAIN*), certain that in these early days he would be able to find a place to stay.[16] It should be remembered that at this time, although resistants like the de Vomécourt brothers were trail blazers, they were barely trained amateurs. Bégué was quickly put in touch with two of Hymans' friends in Châteauroux: the garage owner Marcel Fleuret, 86, rue de la Couture, Châteauroux, and then the chemist Henri Renan, 54, rue des Marins, Châteauroux – both Socialists. Renan quickly became the first SOE letter-box in France, and Bégué radioed his address to London during his first transmission on 9 May. At Bégué's suggestion, the system of personal messages (*Messages*

Personnels) – simple phrases broadcast by the BBC at a set time informing agents when drops of men and supplies were due and comprehensible only to the recipients – was introduced during the summer that followed. Hymans and Bégué recruited more letter boxes, including one with Dr Pierre Samuel, and sought out suitable dropping grounds in the area.

OPERATION FAÇADE (AUGUST–SEPTEMBER 1941)

On the night of 6/7 August 1941, Jacques (*field name VALIANT operational code name LEVÉE*) and Gilbert Turck (1911–2012) (alias Capt. Georges

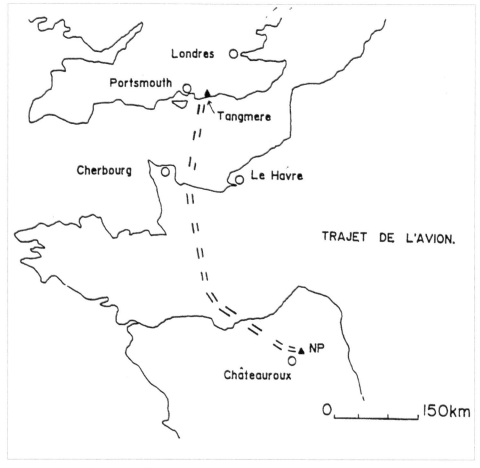

Map of Lysander flight path. Among family papers, provenance unknown

Christophe Tunmer of the Canadian Army, field name CHRISTOPHE), formerly the liaison officer of the *Deuxième Bureau* (part of the French Secret Service), were parachuted blind into France north-west of Montluçon (OPERATION THEOREM/VALIANT) by pilot Sergeant R. E. Austin. John Nesbitt-Dufour wrote that he accompanied some Whiteley drops including the one carrying Jacques. They were dropped from one of SOE's Whitley Mk Vs, at 01.54 hours, but due to a navigational error, Turck missed the landing area, landed badly and well away from Jacques – who looked for him in vain – and lay there unconscious until dawn when he was found by local peasants and handed over to the French police. Amazingly, he was released after interrogation, but too late to be of any use in the area so he made for Marseilles where he installed himself until October in the Villa des Bois.[17] Jacques, too, landed on rough ground, some twelve miles away from the drop zone, near Saint-Désiré in the Allier, 25km north-west of Montluçon but despite being badly cut and bruised, he managed to walk to the pre-arranged rendezvous, where he was met by Bégué. Subsequently, reception parties aimed to be – but were not always – ready and waiting for a drop.

With hindsight, it seems a little odd that Jacques was chosen for this mission. On the one hand, he was bilingual and had friends and relatives all over France, and somehow, he had, despite his height, made his way through France after the chaos of June 1940. But on the other hand, he knew a lot about the workings of SOE and its HQ which would have been extremely valuable to the Germans, all of which he could well have revealed under torture. Moreover, his superiors frowned upon his interest in French politics and must have been aware that his own political views were not only right-wing, but extremely so, for he was an avowed royalist and a former *camelot du roi* (*Des Royalistes dans la Resistance* by Francois-Marin Fleutot, pp. 283–284). It was also common knowledge that he was not – at first at least – a supporter of de Gaulle. But MI5 had not found anything against him when they debriefed him after his return from Spain, and it seems that he carried out his appointed task – in a socialist region of France, among socialist deputies and others – in an exemplary fashion. A minute dated 24 July 1941 records Sporborg (see previously) 'replacing Jacques temporarily by a trainee'. He wrote that as a general principal members of headquarters should not be allowed to go into the field but that Jacques' special qualifications and

Simple map of France showing the demarcation line between the occupied and unoccupied zones [Wiki]

the unusual circumstances of the present case made it a suitable instance for an exception.[18]

A memorandum of 6th Sept set out the main aims of FAÇADE for Jacques:

1   To contact possible organisers in France.
2   To make arrangements for finance.
3   To find W/T operators.
4   To obtain up-to-date identity documents, demobilization certificates, birth certificates, ration cards and coupons etc. for copying.
5   To prepare the way for Virginia Hall (1906-82; code names MARIE and

HECKLER), an American national working as an agent for Section F who would be dropped into Vichy France some time after 23 August 1941 and, posing as a reporter on the staff of the *New York Post*, continue her espionage activities until the Allied invasion of North Africa in December 1942 (OPERATION TORCH).

6   To arrange for fishing boats for the exfiltration of agents to submarines.

7   To find reliable couriers.

8   To make contact with Georges Bégué and Pierre de Vomécourt.

Left on his own, but armed with a list of people provided by Hymans, not all of whom he would have time to see,[19] Jacques travelled all over un-occupied France, carrying out the above tasks to the best of his abilities. Immediately after his return to England, on 6 September, he wrote two memoranda about his time in France. In the first, he assessed the extent to which he had achieved his eight pre-set goals:

He had contacted 'safe' people, notably Jean Laurent of the Banque de l'Indo-Chine, to ensure a supply of francs; he had identified three possible W/T operators; he had put together a valuable collection of up-to-date documents; he had contacted the management of *Les Filles de Paris* at their Lyons office to ascertain their feelings and prepare the way for Virginia Hall's (1906–1982) arrival;[20] he had found two reliable couriers and arranged for others whose names had been suggested by friends; he had made arrangements for fishing-boats to in- and exfiltrate agents and amassed useful personnel to and from British submarines in the areas around the Mediterranean ports of Sète and Marseilles; he had contacted various French organisations and interviewed a number of leading French public men, including Paul Boncour (1873–1972), the socialist politician who had been Premier of France from December 1932 to January 1933; and he had contacted the *Deuxième Bureau*, who had offered him copies of all their files and documents and, more particularly, information on the workings of the censorship system and the general impact of British broadcasts to France, with specific suggestions about broadcasts to agriculturists. In the second memorandum, Jacques reported on his attempts to link up with elements of the Resistance movement that was beginning to grow up piecemeal and haphazardly all over France and attempted to assess their strength and potential.

Secondly, following Turck's accident and capture, Jacques made straight for Marseilles, where he met old friend and former liaison officer with then BEF, Erik Wesberge, (see note 5, Ch. 2), whom he asked to help him contact former colleagues. Wesberge currently held an official teaching post in Marseilles, covering for an absent colleague, but once that colleague returned, he, Wesberge, would be transferred to Orléans where his excellent official cover would enable him to start organising. For the present he was in contact with Michel Lurot, James de Pourtalès, Sauverwein, Pierre Maurette, and his own brother who lived near Caen. Their cover names were provided, and it was promised that Wesberge would be financed by Georges Turck (with whom Jacques had left 30,000 francs and who would also confirm the regions in which the above contacts could most usefully work).

Jacques also reported that through Max Hymans he had made contact with Dr Elie Levy (or Levi; 1896 – 24 January1945†, during one of the infamous "marches of death" from KZ-Auschwitz-Birkenau), code-name LOUIS, who would prove very useful in the future as a leading member of the Spindle circuit around Antibes.[21]

Among the people whom Jacques met were four men who were destined play a significant part in the secret war. There was Philippe Liewer (see note 5, Ch. 2), who was responsible for the SALESMAN circuit around Rouen.[22] Liewer's file states that he was recruited in Nice in September 1941 by Captain George Langelaan (1908–72), but Jacques may have known him from his time as a liaison officer with the BEF in 1939/40 and made the initial approaches during his visit, leaving Langelaan to finalise things.[23] Then there was Jean Bouguennec (1912–1943/44†, probably in KZ-Buchenwald), (*code name FRANCIS GAREL*) who built up BUTLER circuit in the Sarthe area. The third man was Robert Lyon (1897–1986) (*code name ADRIEN*), who was Head of the ACOLYTE circuit which was active in the final liberation of the Roanne region. Finally, there was Jean Pierre-Bloch (1905–99), the former Socialist Deputy for the Aisne who lived at Villamblard near Bergerac and who, with his wife, Gabrielle Sadourny (1908–96) – 'GABY', would also prove invaluable to SOE. Here is Bloch's account of his first meeting with Jacques in Châteauroux, in August 1941 (*Mes Jours Heureux*, 1947, pp. 176–184):

I will never forget the day in Châteauroux at the end of August [1941] when I was introduced to someone called 'Jacques'[…] A message was waiting for me at Villamblard from Max Hymans: 'Come and see me. I've got something to tell you.' I rushed onto the Périgord–Paris express. Max was on the platform at Châteauroux. When he caught sight of me, he shouted:

'Good day, old friend; I'm going to introduce you to my sister-in-law.' And taking my arm, he whispered: 'It's Jacques, one of the top men in London. He's expecting us.'

I was quite overcome. Such a tide of thoughts, questions, exclamations crowded inside me on the way, that I was almost speechless. In the Square, opposite the 'Hôtel du Faisan' [which is still there, though hardly 4-star, having survived bombing during the war], a young man was waiting for us, apparently unconcerned about the harsh August sun. Tall, very handsome. Max introduced us.

'Pierre. Jacques. You need to talk. I'll leave you together.' So Jacques and I began a long walk through the quiet streets of Châteauroux.

'I've come to investigate a particular point, Jacques said, that of landing grounds for parachuting in both arms and men. I need you for this question'.

'I'm at your disposal; but there are also a great many things that I can learn from you. Do you know de Gaulle?'

'Yes. Do you know any suitable grounds in your region?' (De Guélis was rather evasive when de Gaulle's name came up and his lack of enthusiasm would work against him later in the war.)

'I'll have to search. What sort of man is he?'

'An admirable man. Do you think that you will be able to receive planes in the Dordogne soon? All our organisation is ready.'

'I believe I can already point out a site to you. What are they saying about the landings in London?'

'We will drop radios, arms and sometimes men.'

Hôtel du Faisan

In the end we both burst out laughing.

'We can't talk about it all at the same time. I'll give you all the news you want, but then we must consider the question of landing grounds. There is something I want to bring to your notice straight away, before we go any further. You must realise that you risk death, if not worse.'

'Yes, I know. But I agree.'

'Don't give me your reply straight away. We will meet again, if you agree, at 11 o'clock, Place de l'Église. Think about it, you can say no …'

At 11 o'clock precisely I saw Jacques emerge from a street, a cigarette in his mouth, (an English cigarette, with a forgotten aroma) and a book under his arm. (*Pierre-Bloch*, 1946, pp. 176–181 author's translation)

If Jacques really was smoking an English cigarette, it was a serious lapse on the part of a former conducting officer, since SOE took great pains to make sure that their agents wore nothing and had nothing on them that could give them away. Clothes for F Section were either originals or made in the French way, with every detail meticulously copied, and before agents were flown out of an airfield, someone would, with the assistance of the conducting officer, check them for flaws in their disguise. But it was still early days and perhaps not all the checks had been put into place.

Despite this potentially lethal lapse, Pierre Bloch agreed to co-operate, and Jacques squeezed his arm. Then, as they strolled along, smoking, the Socialist and the Royalist discussed their beliefs. Pierre-Bloch asked Jacques about the book by the right-wing thinker Charles Maurras (1868–1952) that he was carrying. In return, Jacques explained that he had once belonged to the right-wing French youth movement known as *Les Camelots du Roi* (founded 1908), that he had broken with Maurras' *Action Française*, and that he had been influenced by the Historian Jacques Bainville (1879–1936), the author of *Les Conséquences le la Paix* (1920).[24] The two men then came to an agreement on future parachute drops so that the only thing left to do was to locate suitable landing grounds. Bloch asked:

'Can you come and examine them yourself?'
'Of course. In exactly eight days time I shall be at
Villamblard. By the way, you will need a name. What do
you want to be called?'
'How about Gabriel? My wife is called Gaby.'

'Right. I will ask for Gabriel on behalf of Max'
(*Pierre Bloch*, 1946, p.180 author's translation)

A week later, Pierre-Bloch met Hymans at Villamblard to look for suitable landing grounds. After some perambulations they chose a clearing at a *lieu-dit* called Lagudal, near Beleymas, 13km from Villamblard, as the place which, as Pierre-Bloch put it in his book, would have the honour of receiving the first parachute drop of arms in France. Three agents landed successfully, and after being received by Pierre-Bloch and his friends, Edouard Dupuy and Albert Rigoulet, they met up at the house of Henri Renan, in Châteauroux, where they found Jacques, Bégué and two new English arrivals.

During the course of that evening, they mapped out the whole plan of action for unoccupied France, where the collaborationist Intelligence Service was already highly organised. Jacques then informed them that they would be joined by sabotage specialists, who had to be hidden for several days before being found work on farms, and explained that Pierre-Bloch's group would be informed by a 'personal message' on the radio when the drop was imminent. In this instance, the message, transmitted from Bush House – '*Gabriel vous envoie ses amitiés*' – would indicate that the mission would take place on the same night, when the moon was full, followed by the message – '*Gabriel va bien*'– to indicate that the ETA (estimated time of arrival) would be midnight. Finally, Jacques also told them that the first drop would bring them three agents, two radios, two million francs and some letters, and that the arms would arrive with the second drop. The relevant 'personal message' was transmitted from Bush House, London, on 2 October 1941 and the following eight evenings. At last, on about 10 October, Pierre-Bloch heard '*Gabriel va bien*', and two years later he learnt that the delay had been caused by London's worst fog for a century. Thus began SOE's infiltration of agents and material all over France.

Jacques' meeting with Pierre-Bloch identified other useful contacts in the area, he reported, such as Dr Dupuis, the leading local physician, and the local landowner, Princesse de Caraman Chimay, both of whom had considerable influence in the locality of Châteauroux. It rapidly transpired they already had at their disposal a small but particularly well-picked organisation which could be extended at any time using the system of cells and which was capable of acting across the line that divided occupied from unoccupied France.[25] At Châteauroux, Max Hymans would operate under his real name, but as he was Jewish, the titular head of the organisation would be Auguste Chantraine (1896–1945† KZ-Mauthausen) (*code name OCTAVE*), a leading local farmer and well-situated as a Resistance leader as he had been the Mayor of Tendu (Indre) since 1936. Hymans also declared his intention of recruiting two prominent politicans. The first was Robert Mauger (1891–1956), the radical socialist deputy for Loir-et-Cher 1932–42, the Mayor of Contres (Loir-et-Cher), and one of the eighty deputies who, in 1940, had refused to vote in favour of the measure that gave full power to Marshal Pétain. The second was Paul Ramadier (1888–1961), a well-known socialist politician who had been deputy for the Aveyron 1928–40 and who would become France's Premier from January to November 1947.

Jacques also reported that he had made contact with his old acquaintance Captain Merrick (MERIC), General Brooke's former liaison officer (see note 5, Ch. 2). He was now a Director of the Marseilles-based Compagnie Cyprien-Fabre, founded in 1881, and one of France's most important shipping companies.[26] He had already done much to help British evaders to get back to England, and was ready to help some more, 'inconspicuously if possible'. Jacques' report also said that Pierre de Vomécourt now 'had his headquarters in Paris where he was developing a very sound organisation' (*code-name AUTOGIRO*) and wished to attach ALBERT (Roger Cottin-Burnett [b. 1903]) and GASTON (Noël Burdeyon) to himself as they were finding that without relations and influence, they could not work up any organisation in their own districts. Jacques also learnt that De Vomécourt's brother, Philippe, using the cover name of CLAUDE, was working from Limoges and covering No. 14 Zone, as his family had a home called Bas Soleil near St Léonard de Noblat, not far from Limoges. De Vomécourt was also able to cross the internal French frontier in No. 4 Zone, since he had a fairly important position in the French railways and was daily obtaining enlistments from and action among the *cheminots* (French railwaymen). De Vomécourt's second brother, Jean de Vomécourt (OLIVIER), also had an active organisation in the forbidden occupied zone that covered an area stretching from the internal frontier in the south to around Laon in the north. He had made the necessary plans for all railway communications with Germany to be cut on orders from England, whereupon Philippe would cut all communications between the internal frontier and the sea on a line roughly from Limoges to Rochefort.

Jacques said he had particular confidence in two of the French national Resistance organisations with which he made contact. The first had its HQ in Lyons and its Chief was Georges Oudards. This organisation, which covered unoccupied France and whose influence stretched far into the occupied zone, was behind the clandestine anti-German newspaper *Les petites ailes de la France*. The second organisation, to which Jacques had been introduced by Dominique de Lesseps, had its HQ at Marseilles and one of its chiefs was Jean Bardanne (b. 1894) (*code name HUBERT*), then of the CARTE Circuit, who currently edited L'Actualité from Marseilles (see map on page 66).

EXFILTRATION AND AFTER (SEPTEMBER 1941)

His mission completed, arrangements were made for Jacques to be flown out of France on the night of 5/6 September 1941 and for another agent, Major Gérard Henri Morel (PAULOT) (see note 5, Ch. 2) to be flown in.[27] This was the pick-up first operation by the newly-formed No. 138 (Special Duties) Squadron (see note 12) Lysander piloted by Flight Lieutenant John ('Whippy') Nesbitt-Dufort.[28] It was to land on 'les Grands Peyroux' – a piece of open ground of which 'Whippy' had an aerial photograph – that was just to the north-east of the crossroads above the hamlet of Villefavant, in the commune of Neuvy-Pailloux between Châteauroux and Issoudun (see map on p. 74). But just as Jacques was getting ready to leave his hotel, probably in Châteauroux, and head out towards the landing ground with his assistant GAREL (and recruit Jean Bouguennec), the French police arrived to make a spot check on everyone's papers. As no-one was permitted to leave before the entire check had been completed, the two agents, aware that precious minutes were passing, had to remain calm. But once the police had left, the pair leapt onto their bicycles and pedalled madly through the night until they reached the crossroads, where Jacques, in haste and slightly behind schedule, selected the wrong field, the '*Pièce des Fontaines*', just to the north-west of the crossroads above Villefavant and a fraction nearer to Neuvy-Pailloux. But 'Whippy' had already arrived, and finding no-one at the pre-arranged site, had risked circling for fifteen minutes. He was just about to head for home when

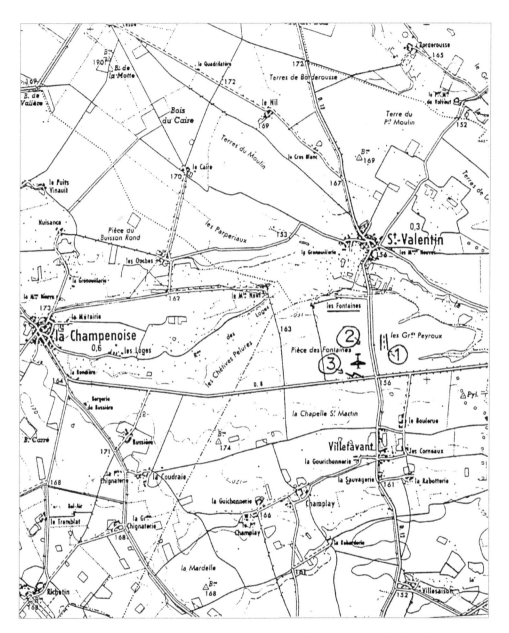

The Rendezvous near La Champenoise for 5/6 September 1941. **1** marks the place where John Nesbitt-Dufort should have landed; **2** marks the place where he actually landed; **3** marks the place from which he managed to take off.

he caught sight of the correct signal, a G, being flashed from a field over to his right. So when Jacques heard the Lysander, he hastily laid out his landing lights and guided 'Whippy' down – but into the wrong field which was much too small and ended in a row of trees, making take-off difficult.[29] 'Whippy' later reported that the subsequent take-off, after a mere four minutes on the ground, was a nightmare. The Lysander went through some telegraph wires which put its wireless out of action; on the way home he had to 'corkscrew' – perform a violent diving turn – in order to elude two German night-fighters; and fog greeted them at Tangmere, where they got down safely with some of the snagged wires

Jean Boughennec (F)

still dangling from the aircraft. On landing, they repaired to the SOE's Tangmere Cottage (see note 12), where Jacques recounted his dash through the night (see Verity, 1978, *We Landed by Moonlight*, pp. 39–40).[30]

In the aftermath of the operation, London sent a series of telegrams dated 5–10 September 1941 congratulating Jacques on his arrival and informing Bégué of Jacques' safe return. Bégué reported that the operation (FACADE) had been successful apart from damage to one bicycle and the noise caused in the locality by the Lysander's landing.[31] But he also told London that they could have the fullest confidence in their special envoy. In a memoir after the war, Begué remarked that luckily Jacques only stayed in France a month as he was a bit of a nuisance wanting to chat, and eat and drink well. (72 AJ/40/11/piece 7C)

AFTERMATH AND CONCLUSION

Jacques' reconnaissance and recruitment work in the Châteauroux area was continued when four other agents were parachuted on 10 October 1941 as the CORSICAN MISSION and met by Bégué and Hymans. This mission consisted of Captain Clement Max Jumeau, Jack Beresford Hayes, Jean le Harivel and Daniel Turberville. But the circuit that Jacques had helped these men to establish did not last long and on 20 October 1941 and the following days, the French police arrested a dozen agents at George Turck's house near Marseilles, most of whom would, however, escape from Mauzac[32] during a mass break-out on 16 July 1942.

Among those captured was Jean Pierre-Bloch who was asked, during his subsequent interrogation, if he knew 'Guélis', to which he replied in the affirmative. He was then shown a photo of him. Knowing Jacques to be in London but sick at heart, he replied that he recognised him. Bégué, also captured and interrogated, later reported that the interrogator from the *Bureau de la Surveillance du Territoire* wanted to know who Bodington and Jacques were and had a photo of the latter.[33] Jacques' name also figures in the interrogations of several of the other prisoners, some of whom clearly told their captors untrue stories in order to muddy the waters further. Pierre-Bloch told his captors that Jacques had given him a million francs on 12 October, to be handed to CHRISTOPHE (one of Turck's code names), and a woman calling herself Georgette Dunais claimed that Jacques was her lover and that she knew nothing about his being an agent. But it is clear that the Vichy authorities must have been aware of Jacques' activities from the outset and were trying to find information on his whereabouts; and he may even have been tried in his absence by the *Tribunal d'État* in Lyons although there appears to be no record.[33]

But for all the uncertainties and loose ends left by his mission, Jouanneau 1995 (see Ch. 2) suggests that Jacques' visit to the Indre was important for several reasons. First, it indicated that if the fight against Vichy and the Nazis were to be successfully carried out, it required co-operation between people of very different political views. Second, it proved that such co-operation was possible and that those on the ground could be encouraged by the presence of a French officer from SOE's London HQ to step up their efforts and activities.

Vichy clearly had an inkling that Jacques was somehow involved in clandestine activities. The interrogations of the captured agents support this view. Given that he came from the French *petite noblesse* it wouldn't have taken much research to find that he had dual nationality and was a resident of England. That the Vichy authorities had his photo in their possession along with Bodington's[34] suggests that someone had been following his activities. The possibility that he had been condemned in his absence has not been proved, but the interrogations of the captive agents certainly prove that Vichy was aware of his involvement in clandestine affairs in the ZNO (Unoccupied zone).

After his return from France, Jacques worked mainly in the London HQ of F Section between September 1941 and November 1942. He would have been kept busy conducting aspiring agents to their courses as well as briefing agents before their departure. Pierre Bloch remembered being met by Jacques on his arrival in Britain.

Jacques was awarded a secret MBE on 9 March 1942 for his work during FACADE and there was a suggestion from Dr Hugh Dalton that he should receive it in private audience with King George VI (see Jacques' personal file). However, the Windsor Archives are sure this did not happen, that the appointment was dated 9 March 1942 and the investiture took place on 12 December 1944 (RA ENC/index/BE). See also an explanatory letter from the Central Chancery of the Orders of Knighthood of 22 February 2012. He is wearing the ribbon of the order in an undated official photograph and there are mentions of him being seen wearing it well before the official investiture date. It appears that he was entitled to wear the ribbon of the Order from 9 March 1942 but had to wait until his investiture in December 1944 to wear the medal. So much for secrecy!

Between 4 and 24 April 1942, about the time he was promoted to Major, he was in Gibraltar briefing agents who were due to to be infiltrated into France. If he was sent on secret missions elsewhere during this period, the records are silent until August 1942.

OPERATION JUBILEE
THE DIEPPE RAID 19 AUGUST 1942

This disastrous raid on the French coast was designed to co-ordinate naval, air and land forces in a combined operations attack, as advised by Louis Mountbatten.

The goal was to probe German defences on the French coast. It was the first Canadian Army engagement in the war in Europe which was to prove a disaster for them and incurred heavy losses. The British also lost heavily, with the RAF losing 106 planes and the Canadian Air Force losing 13.

In the National Archives (ADM199/1079) the naval operation orders give a list of parties to assemble on 10 August at Signal Staff House:

Special Intelligence Party, War Office	10
Inter-allied commando	7
RAF Liaison officers	4
RAF Seargeant	1
SOE	9
MEW	1

The SOE party was led by Major Peter Harratt (HS9/59/2), and among them were Jacques and Teddy Bisset. Jacques never set foot on shore.

The party were attached to Canadian forces and some were there only as observers while others had various objectives on shore. Peter Harratt certainly went ashore and some reports say he was wounded, but there is a photograph of Peter Harratt and Teddy Bisset on board a ship returning from Dieppe.

All in all this mission proved very costly with over 3,000 Canadian casualties for little gain.

As Guy Liddell of MI5 commented in his diaries (*op cit*): 'The operation seems to have been somewhat costly, but no doubt valuable experience has been gained.'

(For more information consult the many sites devoted to this subject)

FOOTNOTES

[1] Letter from Sir Brooks Richards to Major Everett regarding Cathays Cemetery Heritage Trail on 23 March 1996. It is no surprise that no written record of this meeting can be found among the Churchill papers or anywhere else. All Churchill's 'favourite' lady agents claim to have had regular contact with him!

[2] Gielgud certainly interviewed André Simon, who, despite some disquiet about his lack of discretion, joined SOE two weeks after being commissioned in the RAF; see Simon's and de Guélis' personal files (HS9/1362/2 and HS9/630/10).

[3] Code name Roger, one of SOE's most successful agents who, although a conscientious objector at the start of the war, joined the organisation in 1942 as a result of the death of his younger brother Pieter on 30 March 1941 while flying as a Sergeant Observer with 101 Squadron, RAF. His jockey circuit in southern France, which finally involved more than 10,000 people, played a major part in the liberation of that region by enabling the Allied armies to advance rapidly up the Rhône Valley. He also organised armed Resistance in the Vercors area. Private communication to the author.

[4] Jean le Harivel, field name Georges 25 [all wireless operators were 'George'], operational code *Hiccup/Hoquet*. Phone conversation with the author.

[5] The route de Guélis gave Peter Churchill was via Port Vendres near Collioure, above Banyuls. via Cerbere, Port Bou, Colera ending up at Llança where a train took workmen to Barcelona.

[6] Vera Atkins joined F Section in February 1941; Colonel Buckmaster joined SOE on 17 March 1941 and worked as Section F's Information Officer until his promotion in September 1941. For more on Vera Atkins see the excellent *A life in Secrets* by Sara Helm, 2005.

[7] Code name *Thermomètre*, he would be the medical officer with de Guélis during Operation Tilleul in 1944.

[8] See Bernie Ross' informative web-site *Training SOE Saboteurs in World War Two* (last updated 17 February 2011). It seems likely that de Guélis combined his own training with his role as conducting officer. His file does not elaborate.

[9] Field name Jacquot, operational code Calder.

[10] Apparently de Guélis had difficulty parachuting because of his size and his parachute had a 36ft canopy instead of the normal 32ft one. George Connerade confirmed this in a conversation with the author. For more information on SOE parachute training at Ringway, see article by Andrew Defty, University of Salford for a Study Group on Intelligence, Winter 1992/3. By 1940, the Parachute Training Unit, which had been at RAF Henlow since 20 September 1925, employed 270 staff to repair and pack over 200 parachutes per week.

[11] The name of the unit that was first used for work with both SIS and the SOE. On 25 August 1941, No. 138 (Special Duties) Squadron was formed from No. 1419 Flight, and serviced both SIS and SOE until the formation of No. 161 Squadron, when in general, No. 138 serviced SOE and 161 SIS. From 25 August 1941 to 1 January 1942 SOE flights departed from RAF Newmarket; from 1 January to 14 March 1942 SOE flights departed from RAF Stradishall, near Bury St Edmunds; and from 14 March 1942 SOE flights departed from the specially constructed, secret airfield at Tempsford, in Bedfordshire. The RAF's No. 161 Squadron, (Special Duties)

began operations in February 1942, just before RAF Tempsford became operational.

[12] See Georges Bégué's personal file HS9/115/21. Throughout the war, the SOE made use of a clandestine base in Tangmere Cottage, just opposite the main gate; Tangmere being the base from which agents were landed or picked up by Lysander. It was here returning agents repaired to relax and have a meal. See also *The French Resistance in Sussex* by Barbara Bertram,1995.

[13] During its existence, F Section lost 91 men and 13 women agents, most of whom died or were executed in German prisons and concentration camps. For detailed information on those who worked for Section F and those who died while working for SOE and its attendant RAF units, Google 'Special Forces Roll of Honour' and 'Special Operations Executive SOE 1940–1945: French Section' and 'Liste des Agents du SOE'.

[14] Valençay was chosen as the site for the SOE Memorial that was unveiled on 6 May 1991, the 50th anniversary of the SOE's first drop into France, in the presence of The Queen Mother.

[15] Max Hymans' family papers with thanks to his son Daniel Hymans.

[16] Bégué was an engineer by profession and had studied Engineering at the University of Hull. He also had an English wife. After getting out of France at Dunkirk, he became a Sergeant in the Royal Signals and was rapidly recruited to SOE's F Section. All three de Vomécourt brothers were active in the Resistance – Philippe de Vomécourt had several meetings with de Guélis in Châteauroux – he had an estate near Limoges called Bas Soleil. (See *Who Lived to See the Day* by Philippe de Vomécourt. p. 69.)

[17] He stayed on in France and was arrested for the second time in July 1942 at Saint-Germain-des-Prés. He spent the rest of the war in French prisons (Fresnes) or German concentration camps (KZ-Buchenwald, KZ-Dora and KZ-Bergen-Belsen) and was finally liberated by the British in April 1945. See the on-line 'SOE Archives' and the French Wikipedia article on 'Gilbert Charles Georges Turck'.

[18] HS7/218 p.1267.

[19] HS7/220.

[20] She later worked for OSS and ended the war, highly decorated, as the USA's foremost woman spy (see *Nouzille, L'Espionne: Virginia Hall, une Americaine dans la Guerre*, 2008).

[21] Peter Churchill was sent there on his first and second missions, as was the gay agent Denis Rake (see *Rake's Progress* by Denis Rake, 1968, pp. 94–100. See also Nigel Perrin's very useful website on Denis Rake).

[22] See Nigel Perrin's very informative website on Philippe Liewer.

[23] See Philippe Liewer's's personal file HS9/923/4.

[24] For more detailed information on these topics, Google Charles Maurras, Jacques Bainville, the author of *Les Conséquences de la paix* (1920), *Action Française* and the *Camelots du Roi* (who were expected to sell the newspaper). During the Occupation, Maurras began to publish the newspaper *Action Française* once again and supported the Vichy regime. Quite apart from the ideological differences separating Socialists like Pierre-Bloch and Max Hymans from the right-wing, monarchist *Action Française*, the latter group was strongly anti-semitic. In contrast, both Max Hymans and Pierre-Bloch were Jewish, and Pierre-Bloch had been active in the fight against Anti-semitism since the 1930s and continued to be so after the war, when the periodical *Action Française* was banned.

[25] HS7/220.

[26] Since 1933 the Compagnie Générale de Navigation à Vapeur.

[27] Morel's arrival at F Section had been long and tortuous. A liaison officer with the BEF in Spring 1940, he had been captured at Dunkirk, where he was found lying on the ground so ill and exhausted that the Germans did not think he would live and released him. He got to Spain and determined to reach England, took a boat to Brazil and returned thence to Portugal, where he managed to contact British Intelligence. He joined SOE, but his subsequent experiences were no less gruelling and his health was ruined for good.

[28] He was called 'Whippy' because he had once crash-landed at Whipsnade, and his Lysander had a large red question mark painted on the fuselage, which was black.

[29] Once on the ground, Morel jumped out and ran towards the trees, finding on the way a sack that de Guélis had left on the ground, Morel picked it up and disappeared. It contained presents of cognac and perfume. The incident would later be used as the opening and closing shots in the documentary film *Now it Can be Told* (produced in 1944 by the RAF Film Production Unit; first screened in 1946). Now available as a DVD in the Imperial War Museum's Official Collection. The small fields and hedges have long disappeared and where the field meets the road the site looks more like a prairie with an industrial building. It is hoped that one day a stele will mark this historic landing.

[30] A Lysander piloted by J. Nesbitt Dufort crashed near Issoudun on 28/29 April 1942, returning from operation BERYL, due to low fuel. While an attempt was being made to tow it away, it was hit by a train on a railway crossing and completely destroyed. See: *Flights of the Forgotten*, p. 44, *We Landed by Moonlight*, pp. 171, 214–216 and harringtonmuseum.org.uk/aircraft lost on Allied Forces Special Duty Ops.

[31] HS9/115/21.

[32] A commemorative stele at Lagudal records this drop, when four officers in the British Army, all trained sabotage instructors, landed there: Clément Marc Jumeau (1914–44†, Berlin, as a result of maltreatment when in German captivity) (code names ROBERT, REPORTER), Jack Beresford Hayes (b. 1904) (code names VICTOR, HELMSMAN), the newly married Jean le Harival (191–2006) (field name GEORGE XXV, operational code HOCQUET, HICCUP) and Daniel Turberville (b. 1915) (code names DANIEL, DIVINER). Jumeau, Hayes and le Harival survived the drop and made it to Marseilles to link up with Georges Turck, but were arrested and ended up in prison at Mauzac, from which they escaped on 16 July 1942. But Turberville, who was dropped last, missed the rendezvous point by 12 km and was arrested by French police on 11 October. But he, too, managed to escape when being taken by train to Lyon and made it back to England.

[33] Nicholas Bodington (1904–1974), a senior member of F Section throughout the war. According to Bodington's PF (HS9/171/1) at the National Archives, the Gestapo had his photo and description.

[34] Interrogations by Vichy of captured agents in Max Hyman's papers.

4

DE GUÉLIS AND THE MASSINGHAM
MISSION (JANUARY–OCTOBER 1943)

*An active and effective officer in his present
capacity, with considerable charm of manner
and telling personality. He is well adapted
to his present functions; he has recently been
posted abroad, which I hope will deepen his
sense of responsibility and broaden his
judgement.*

Major R. E. Brook – June to December 1942

*His knowledge of military affairs is limited
but [he] has shown particular aptitude in
liaison with the French authorities from
the political point of view. A capable
officer with particular knowledge of the
French and French affairs.*

Douglas Dodds-Parker – August 1943
(Comments in de Guélis's personal file) at the National Archives

THE POLITICAL SITUATION IN NORTH AFRICA (NOVEMBER/DECEMBER 1942–FEBRUARY 1943)

On 7 November 1942, two secret cipher telegrams were sent from Gibraltar to
'MASSINGHAM', the official code name for ISSU No. 6, symbol AMF, the newly

established SOE base at Guyotville, just west of Algiers. The first announced the departure on 8 November of V and W who were to wait for X, Y and Z, who hoped to leave on 12 November. The second put names to the letters: V = Major de Guélis, W = Squadron-Leader Green, X = Lieutenant-Colonel Keswick, Y = Lieutenant-Colonel Glyn and Z = Major Hepner.[1]

In the wake of OPERATION TORCH, Jacques was posted to Algiers, where he arrived from Cairo on 5 December 1942 as a member of MASSINGHAM, the advanced operational base for the infiltration of agents into Southern France in preparation for the eventual landings there (August 1944). Soon after his arrival, Jacques was able to wire his cousin Val Barbier, who would arrive himself in Algiers in February 1943 and stay on after Jacques' departure as a valued member of the team, the news of their cousin Eric Duncan's death 'in a most gallant action' at Oran.[2] By December 1942, SOE personnel were occupying a group of villas at Cape Matifou, and their CO was Colonel J. W. Munn, with Lieutenant-Colonel David Keswick as his deputy and Jacques as GSO2 of the local French Section. One of their officers was Captain Michael Gubbins, the son of General Gubbins, who would be killed, aged twenty-two, serving with SOE near Monte Cassino on 6 February 1944.

Douglas Dodds-Parker, who had known Jacques from Oxford and Baker Street, was appointed MASSINGHAM's Operations Officer, arriving in Gibraltar on the day after the Allied landings, and flying on to Algeria (Dodds-Parker, 1983, *Setting Europe Ablaze*, pp. 111–112) where he arrived in the midst of a very complicated political situation. The pro-Nazi, anglophobe Admiral Darlan was unexpectedly in Algeria, visiting his son who was recuperating after a severe attack of polio, while General de Lattre de Tassigny (1889–1952),[3] who had initiated French military Resistance in Vichy France and was in prison there, had sent messages to the effect that French Resistance would cease while Darlan held any position in Algiers. The Americans were anti-de Gaulle and favoured General Henri Giraud (1879–1949) as Chief of French Forces. After his capture on 19 May 1940, Giraud had been imprisoned in Königstein prison, near Dresden, but made a daring escape on 17 April 1942 and returned to Vichy, France via Switzerland. The Vichy Government wanted him to go back to Germany voluntarily so as not to upset their relations with the Germans, which he refused to do. But because the Americans wanted to install Giraud, rather than de Gaulle, who, one may imagine, was fuming in the wings, as Governor of Algeria and Commander of French Military Forces in North Africa, they arranged for a British submarine, HMS *Seraph*,[4] to pick Giraud up on 5 November 1942, days before the Allied landings in North Africa, and take him to Gibraltar, where he arrived several days later. On landing in Algiers on 9 November, he professed to be astounded when he found Darlan there already and wondered whether he had known about the landings in advance. To complicate matters still further, the French Royalists were involved in plots and machinations to restore the Pretender to the French throne,[5] nor should it be forgotten that Jacques, like many French aristocrats, was a Royalist (see Giraud, 1949, pp. 33, 74, 76–78 and Fleutot, 2000, pp. 283–284). By and large, the North African troops were loyal to Vichy, and Pétain was popular among them, but it had been hoped they would capitulate when Giraud, who had served in North Africa before both world wars, arrived. Instead, they put up stiff Resistance until Darlan ordered a cease-fire in Oran on 10 November and in Morocco on 11 November, after persuading General Eisenhower to agree that he should stay in charge of the Vichyite Administration in North and West Africa. And on 14 November, the American General acquiesced in Darlan's self-nomination as High Commissioner of France in those regions. Understandably, de Gaulle was enraged... again.

On 27 November 1942, Lieutenant-Colonel David Keswick reported to London that Giraud had been side-lined, leaving Darlan and the pro-Vichy faction in control,[6] and by 18 December, Colonel Munn was telling London that the local situation was becoming ever more complicated – 'quite Balkan' in fact – but that General Eisenhower would remove Massingham if it gave any assistance to anti-Darlan or pro-Gaullist elements. So its members were advised to tread very warily indeed.[7]

It was into this cauldron of intrigue, uncertainty and suspicion that Jacques, Royalist and apparently no fan of de Gaulle, was propelled, as Head of F Section, along with Dodds-Parker and Lieutenant-Colonel Keswick – the latter had annoyed the Foreign Office and the Allied authorities in Algiers because of the accuracy of his information. (Sir Douglas Dodds-Parker's papers, Magdalen College, Oxford.) Jacques was primarily concerned with recruiting Frenchmen to train for operations in Corsica and Southern France. In the context of such work, Jacques' not inconsiderable negotiating skills, charm and connections would have been at a premium, and besides, he was, according to Dodds-Parker, adept at sorting out patriot from Vichyite (Dodds Parker, 1983, p.114). Here, at least, his interest in French politics would have been put to good use.

The political situation came to a head on Christmas Eve, 1942. A young French Royalist called Fernand Bonnier de la Chapelle (1922–42), who had been born in Algeria and returned there after the Fall of France, was a member of the monarchist *Corps Franc d'Afrique* under the command of Henri d'Astier de la Vigerie (1897–1952), the organiser of the pro-Allied Putsch in Algiers on 8 November 1942, when 400 poorly-armed patriots seized control of all key buildings and facilitated the Anglo-American landings. The late SOE agent Bob Maloubier (d. April 2015) told the author that a group of young lads, including himself, a certain Colonel (or more likely Capitaine) Sabatier, perhaps brought in by the American anthropologist Carlton Coon as deputy commander of the unit (See Funk, p.266), and Bonnier de la Chapelle, had been discreetly trained in commando tactics by Jacques and other SOE instructors, as well as, it seems, Carlton Coon, of the OSS. (Funk, *The OSS in Algiers*, p. 167 see bibliography.) Maloubier also confirmed that Jacques knew Bonnier de la Chapelle, having been involved in his training. Sabatier and Bonnier de la Chapelle were in charge of the trainees in their camp and both had been issued with .38 pistols. In December, Capitaine Sabatier and Bonnier de la Chapelle came to see Dodds-Parker (who persisted in calling Bonnier, René) and told him that there was a widespread rumour that the Americans had reached an agreement with Darlan and his colleagues which would safeguard their future and, ultimately, lead to a deal with Vichy. They also said that they and many others believed that only de Gaulle – with Allied help – could save France and had reached the conclusion that, because of his record, Dodds-Parker could give a fair assessment of the justification for Darlan's removal (Dodds-Parker, 1983, pp. 115–116). After due consideration, Dodds-Parker told them carefully that his opinion was the same as theirs). Ragueneau, Tournier, Gross and Bonnier de la Chapelle then, according to some accounts, drew straws to decide who was to assassinate Darlan. Bonnier de la Chapelle drew the short straw and, after receiving absolution from the Abbé

Cordier, went to the Palais d'Été in the afternoon of 24 December and shot Darlan twice, killing him. He was apprehended on the spot, quickly tried, and executed on 26 December on the orders of General Giraud, Darlan's replacement. Others, including Abbé Cordier, were arrested, and Capitaine Sabatier was packed off to England via Gibraltar. Speculation ran rife as to who was behind the coup and who had armed the assassin, since his murder weapon had not been the one issued by the SOE; De Gaulle, or even the Comte de Paris (note 5), Giraud wondered, or the British who had concluded that it was in their interest for the Admiral to be eliminated? No wonder Dodds-Parker followed orders and destroyed a large proportion of the MASSINGHAM papers. Jacques had thought that the assassin would just be imprisoned for a while and there was concern at the speed of his execution.[8] During all of this, the British were being watched by the Americans and French Security and had, no doubt, to answer some awkward questions.

After Bonnier de la Chapelle's death, two curious things emerged. First, after being sentenced, he had asked to speak to a policeman and the Commissaire Gardacci was produced. Bonnier told him that the Abbé Cordier knew of the plot and that he himself had thought that he was under the protection of d'Astier de la Vigerie. But Gardacci said nothing about this until after the execution, when a search of his office produced the report. Second, Giraud reported in his memoir that immediately after the execution, the Comte de Paris (note 5), accompanied by an unnamed gentleman, came to see Giraud in order to beg for clemency. On hearing that they were too late, they went on to the main object of their visit – which was to ask Giraud whether he would support the restoration of the monarchy. But Giraud would have none of it, pointing out that, according to the relevant law of 1886, the Comte should not even be on French soil, and sent him packing back to Spanish Morocco (Giraud, 1949, pp. 76–78).

Enter Bob Maloubier, a recruit of Jacques' and a school friend of Bonnier de la Chapelle's at Neuilly. In *Nageurs de Combat*, he describes how he became attached to the French Air Force base at Bizerta before going on to Algiers. He learnt that some French volunteers were being given instruction in commando tactics by the British at Cape Matifou and joined some others, including Fernand Bonnier de la Chapelle and Capitaine Sabatier behind the high walls of an agricultural building. They were put in British battle-dress and issued with Sten sub-machine-guns, firing 9mm pistol ammunition; Maloubier thought that Bonnier de la Chapelle might also have had a SOE hand-gun. Most interestingly, he described one of their instructors, Jacques, as a jovial English Major, gargantuan, with a pipe glued to his mouth, who spoke a very refined French, and he opined that despite his French name, he could have not been more British. Like many other people, Maloubier had no idea of Jacques' French ancestry, as Jacques really was both typically French and English. Moreover, his trainees nicknamed him 'Gargantua'[9] as well as '*Ainsi soit-il*', as Maloubier told the author in a letter of 23 July 2006.

On Christmas Eve 1942, Jacques and other British officers were having a drink in their villa at Cape Matifou when Maloubier erupted into the room and told Jacques that the police had occupied their camp. He went on to relate their conversation: Maloubier, concerned for his safety, wanted Jacques to spirit him and two friends to London to join the RAF. Unfortunately, as Jacques was only interested in recruiting agents for the SOE, he, Maloubier, had to give up his dream of becoming a pilot until much later in his life. But he was sent to London to train as an agent and he became a very effective one, too, and was parachuted into France with Violette Szabo on her second, ill-fated mission.[10]

CORSICA (FEBRUARY–APRIL 1943)

On 17 February 1943, MASSINGHAM transferred to the Club des Pins – now a holiday destination – where its staff set up a larger signal station and where there was more room for parachute training and other outdoor activities. During the first six months of 1943, Jacques made several trips to London. On 9 January he went back there to obtain up-to-date information on the situation in France so that MASSINGHAM'S policy could be better co-ordinated, taking with him two members of *Giraud's Deuxième* Bureau, Captain Lejeune and Lieutenant Lerat. The idea was that SOE would send them first to France, and later back to Algiers, in order to explain to Giraud SOE's set-up and the facilities afforded to the French. On his return, Lejeune sent directives to London, confirming that there would be complete collaboration with the British clandestine services.

In February 1943 Jacques was off again, via Gibraltar, where he put Maloubier and his friend Pierre Raynaud (1921–2010)[11] on a ship bound for Glasgow, where they were met by Teddy Bisset, who would be a member of the TILLEUL

MISSION with Jacques in 1944. The third trip lasted from 24 May to 6 July. It may have been occasioned by Jacques' concern for his wife Beryl who was ill, but Jacques was able to have dinner with Buckmaster while in England.[12] Between visits, Jacques carried on his role as briefing officer and instructor, and he also helped set up a communications system between Corsica and Algiers.

Arriving at MASSINGHAM in February 1943 was Captain George V. (VAL) Barbier, Jacques' cousin (*code name VINCENT BAKER*), a captain in the Royal Signals. He had previously been an SOE conducting and briefing officer and was a qualified teleprinter operator and mechanic with a good knowledge of wireless and air ops. He was 2nd in command of F Country section at MASSINGHAM and handled all details to do with agents in the field and prior to their dispatch, as well as assisting with general planning and communications in the field (HS9/87/2). His personal file called him an exceedingly capable officer.

He remained in Algiers after Jacques' departure and was awarded a *Croix de Guerre*.

Relationships with the HQ of the Allied Forces were delicate and MASSINGHAM was obliged to co-operate with General Eisenhower, the Theatre Commander. But eventually, in February 1943, SOE and the American OSS formed a joint Anglo-American operations mission that was headed by Colonel John Munn until Major Dodds-Parker assumed command in February 1943. So Jacques, who had been working very comfortably with the Giraudist administration in North Africa, even forming friendships which, in other circumstances, might have survived the war,[13] found himself obliged to collaborate with the OSS and Paul[in] Colonna d'Istria (1905–82), without de Gaulle or his intelligence service being consulted, and in August 1943 General Giraud wrote to the (recently promoted) Major-General Gubbins:

> *Mon Général,*
> *Je profite de l'arrivée à Alger du Colonel Keswick, pour vous dire combien je suis heureux de la parfaite harmonie qui règne entre vos services dirigés par les Colonels Keswick, Dodds Parker et le Commandant Gillies d'une part, et les miens dont le Général Ronin est le chef […]*[14]

From mid-December 1942, the Allies in North Africa turned their attention towards the major Mediterranean islands, Corsica, Sardinia and Sicily. Little was known about Resistance groups on the island of Corsica, not least because of its wild and mountainous terrain. But it was believed that Gaullist groups existed in Ajaccio, Corte, Bastia and Calvi and that other oppositional groups existed there, too, ranging from Communists to outright bandits. So between mid-December 1942 and early February 1943, four separate reconnaissance missions were sent onto the island.

On 13 December 1942, i.e. *after* the Allied invasion of North Africa and after the Germans had arranged for nearly 85,000 Italian troops to be sent to Corsica (pop. 220,000) between 11 and 14 November 1941 (*Operation Anton*), but *before* the assassination of Darlan, the French military authorities in North Africa, supported by the Americans, sent the French submarine *Casabianca* to Topiti Bay, where it landed the four-man Mission called PEARL HARBOR.[15] Its leader was Commandant Roger de Saule (b. 1889; alias the Belgian Robert de Schrevel, also known as DUDULE and RENÉ TOURNIER), and he was accompanied by three much younger men – Toussaint Griffi (b. 1910), Pierre Griffi (b. 1914–1943†; executed by firing-squad at Bastia on 18 August 1943) and Laurent Preziosi (1912–2010). It stayed on Corsica until March 1943 and was primarily concerned to assess whether the island could be taken back from the occupying Italians and Germans by a purely French invasion force. At the same time, OSS agent Frederick Brown, briefed by Lieutenant-Colonel Keswick and Jacques and code-named TOMMY accompanied the mission to gather intelligence on possible reception of arms by sea and air. A French source stated that TOMMY was limited to the submarine voyage and supplying radio equipment. Then, on 4 January 1943, the British submarine HMS *Tribune* arrived in the Bay of Cupabia with MISSION SEA URCHIN.[16] Its leader was the Gaullist Fred Scamaroni (SEVERI) (1914–43†), and he was accompanied by James Anthony Jickell (ANDRÉ MEYNARD) and a wireless operator, Henri Hellier. Unfortunately, Scamaroni was betrayed and arrested, and committed suicide in prison rather than talk. Then on 7 February 1943, the three-man MISSION FRÉDÉRIQUE left Algiers in the submarine HMS *Saracen* and was also landed in the Bay of Cupabia.[17] Its leader was the trained agent and wireless operator

Guy Verstraete (alias GUY VERNUGE [1918–43†]) and the other two men were native Corsicans: Antoine Colonna d'Istria (1906–1986), a businessman, and Charles Simon Andrei (1903–43†), a schoolteacher. Andrei and Verstraete were betrayed, captured, tortured and executed by firing-squad at Bastia on 6 July 1943. Antoine Colonna d'Istria, condemned to death *in absentia*, was never caught and like his cousin Paulin, refused any position on the island after the war, going into business instead.[18]

THE BUILD-UP TO THE INVASION OF CORSICA
(APRIL–9 SEPTEMBER 1943)

Although there was a strong spirit of Resistance on the island, it lacked leadership and arms. But on the night of 3/4 April 1943, the British submarine HMS *Trident* brought back to Corsica one of the few men who could provide both, Corsican Paul[in] Colonna d'Istria, code name CESARI, together with two lieutenants. By 1943 Colonna d'Istria had become Deputy to the CO of the *Gendarmerie* in North Africa, and although SOE liked to claim that they had recruited him, he would claim that he had been recruited in January 1943 by a young lawyer at the Court of Appeal in Algiers, Maître Sansonetti, accompanied by a Lieutenant Hostis. They were apparently looking for a 'dare-devil' to send in to Corsica. General Giraud approved the nomination and Jacques, who considered him first-class, was involved in his briefing which proved to be the beginning of a close friendship. This, although all too brief, left Colonna d'Istria with a lasting impression of an extraordinary man who was his '*grand ami et camarade de combat*' ('great friend and comrade in arms'). Was this a clue that they had fought together?[19] Unlike Maloubier, Colonna d'Istria was well aware of Jacques' antecedents.[20] As the new mission was to take over where PEARL HARBOR had left off, it was fitting that *Trident* should begin it by exfiltrating Roger de Saule after eighty-seven days on the island.

Besides CESARI, Colonna d'Istria had other code names which included the real names of his sons and nephews: JEAN-PIERRE, FRANCIS, MAURICE, LEO.[21] Like many Corsicans Cesari had his horoscope cast annually. (Brooks Richards) Cesari had been instructed to appoint himself Head of the Resistance in the whole island and was told to contact all existing groups, appoint local chiefs, make preparations for the reception of arms and explosives by sea and air, ensure that this material could be properly distributed and stored, and see that there was a sound system of communication with Algiers.[22]

Two months later, having travelled the length and breadth of the island, CESARI had performed a near miracle not only by accomplishing the above task but also by persuading all the disparate groups on the island to work together as an effective fighting force. By the end of May 1943 he had become their recognised chief and could claim to have 9,000 men under a single command, organised in cadres

Paulin Colonna d'Istria (1905–82)

throughout the island. To make security as tight as possible, no man knew more than the man immediately above him and each group was kept separate (Gambiez, 1973, p. 152). CESARI himself set great store by disguise: he could be clean-shaven, or badly shaven, with or without a moustache or hat. His adage was that to effect a useful disguise, all one needed to do was change from a beret to a felt hat.[23]

In addition, CESARI had identified about sixty sites for receiving drops of supplies and ammunition in the island's difficult, mountainous terrain. But during this early period, there does not seem to have been a plan for parachuting men onto the island, so that the widespread belief that this is how Jacques arrived there is nearly, but not quite correct. In a letter from a certain Johnny Kempthorne (1919–2001) of SOE to leading seaman Don Miles, the writer claims there was a plan for Jacques, a captive Italian General and himself to be dropped into the Corte area in order to try and persuade the Italians to change sides. But at the last minute, the captive General, who was friendly with General Giovanni Magli (1884–1969), the GOC Italian forces on Corsica, pulled out. This left Jacques and Kempthorne to go on their own and be met by partisans, and the two of them got as far as being fitted with their parachute harness and taking off from Blida, in Algeria, aboard a Halifax from 138 Squadron from Tempsford, according to Kempthorne. But when they were three-quarters of the way to Corsica, the pilot received a message that the weather in the dropping zone had deteriorated and that a large German force was in the area. So the mission was aborted and they returned to Blida. Although Kempthorne's account does not date the Mission,[24] it must have taken place just before the seaborne landings in September and this may explain some reports that Jacques was dropped by parachute into Corsica. The German presence in Corsica had not been large before June 1943 when about 10,000 men, i.e. about a division, were sent across to stiffen the Italian Resistance. Kempthorne then goes on to describe making the subsequent crossing to Corsica in the French submarine *Surcouf* in the company of a French commando of fifty men plus a British Sergeant called Harry Coltman and a wireless operator called Lance Corporal Collins. But in fact, their designated submarine – which could not have been the *Surcouf* because this huge, underwater cruiser had already been sunk, probably by accident, on 18 February 1942 en route to Tahiti via the Panama Canal – left without them and they were taken across instead by the light cruiser/fast destroyer *Terrible*.

Kempthorne's Personal File states that he was a regular soldier in the Scottish Fusiliers. At some stage he was recruited by SOE and left for Algiers on 29 March 1943 and was attached to the Bataillon de Choc from July to the end of August 1943 in order to train them for the Corsican Operation. He then joined the Air Liaison section at MASSINGHAM and apparently took the first SOE party to Corsica on 8 September 1943, remaining there until the end of October.

CESARI sent a report to MASSINGHAM outlining his achievements and it was decided that he should give a fuller report on board a submarine off the coast in early June, i.e. about the time when Jacques was officially made GSO2 for France in MASSINGHAM and head of its 'Country Section' which dealt, in the first instance, with Corsica and Italy (Hutchins and Sheppard, 2004, p. 85). Val Barbier, now also with SOE in Algiers, was on board HMS *Sibyl* for CESARI's debriefing, but as there was enemy activity on shore the Captain decided to return to Algiers taking his passenger, unexpectedly, with him. [HMS *Sibyl* was ordered to patrol the East coast of Corsica on 1 June 1943, had landed two French agents and taken off five on the 9th. See HMS *Sibyl* on-line.] He could not have chosen a better moment since King George VI was visiting Massingham in June 1943 and CESARI was delighted to be presented to him. The King was most impressed with Cesari but did not, as has been reported, decorate him there and then.[25] On 27 June 1943 CESARI returned to Corsica to continue his mission, having profited from his stay in Algiers to beg for more arms and supplies.[26]

Recently, Radio operator Jean Lannou's papers have come into his son's hands (2015) and it appears he was sent to Algiers in 1942–43 and that he had made seven trips to Corsica on the submarine *Casabianca* including the trip which took CESARI back to the island after his visit to Algiers at the time of the King's visit. Casabianca, according to Captain J. L'Herminier in his book *Casabianca*, was detailed to deliver arms, ammunition and supplies to the resistants in Corsica as well as transporting and collecting agents there. Some of these trips were organised by the French 2nd Bureau and some were combined operations with SOE and OSS and as the agents were not usually named it is difficult to to be specific although L'Herminier describes their destination each time in detail. Val Barbier was on one trip on the submarine *Sibyl* so they may have met and it is highly likely that Jacques got to know him and value him in Algiers and then in 1944, asked for him to be included in MISSION TILLEUL (see Chapter 5). Lannou was awarded the King's medal for Courage in the cause of Freedom and his citation states that: '*he subsequently took part in the landings on the island as W/T operator to the Allied Mission between the patriots and the French High Command.*' Before his transfer to England in 1944 he trained clandestine wireless operators in North Africa. It is tempting to think that Lannou accompanied Jacques' group to Corsica but there is no proof, or was he with Kempthorne's mysterious mission some days earlier?

Meanwhile, in Algiers, the French were forming a *Bataillon de Choc*, a commando unit that would use sabotage and explosives, and generally cause panic by targeting convoys, trains, command posts, aerodromes etc. It was based at Staouli, nowadays another holiday resort, and its CO was General Gambiez (1903–89) who took up his post on 22 May 1943 and rapidly recruited about thirty officers and other ranks. The strength of the *Bataillon* soon increased: partly through volunteers, many of whom were escapees via Spain, partly through deserters who had been freed from prison in Algiers, and partly through men who were recruited on the spot by the *Bataillon*'s instructors. The unit was a veritable hotchpotch, in which all arms of the service were represented: pilots without aircraft, sailors without boats, gunners without guns, tankers without tanks and ordinary infantrymen. One if its number was Jacques de Beaumarchais, a future French Ambassador to London (Gambiez, 1973, p. 179 and Dodds Parker, 1983 p. 154).

An *esprit de corps* was soon established and training began. The men were to be lightly armed with Stens and their uniforms were adapted from the one worn by the Americans. But as the American-issue bomber jacket was too light-coloured to be worn at night, it was worn inside-out. Binoculars and maps were in short supply, but some *Blue Guides* of Corsica were unearthed in local bookshops! Specialised three-week training courses were provided for officers by SOE and OSS instructors at the Club des Pins (Gambiez, p. 173). The idea was that after attending such a course, the officers would be able to return to their units and pass on their newly-acquired knowledge to their men. There is no obvious sign of Jacques here but he may well have been involved.

By July, the *Bataillon* was ready for action and had begun to resent the British and US officers whose task it was to monitor them. Agents from the British and US Special Services would frequent the same bars as the members of the *Battaillon* and persist in questioning the men about the unit and its future role (Gambiez, 1973, p.183). One night, a French officer replied that he had such information at his disposal but that it was too sensitive to reveal in a bar. Invited outside, the stool-pigeon was given evidence that the *Battaillon*'s lessons in close combat had been perfectly understood even though French accounts of this period make little of the SOE's role in training the French commandos. Giraud had said that the operation would be French, purely French (Gambiez, p. 173). What does come across very strongly is, however, the way in which the personal and political animosity between de Gaulle and Giraud was poisoning the atmosphere, not only in Algiers but in France and London as well. On 30 May 1943, de Gaulle had moved his HQ from London to Algiers after some histrionics which forced the Allies to issue him with an ultimatum: to go back to the Casablanca Conference, from 14–24 January, 1943 which was convened to plan Allied strategy. De Gaulle initially refused to attend. He saw no useful purpose in his presence in North Africa, as he wrote to General Giraud, 'if his suggestions for his reforms of the French Army weren't adopted'. He rapidly changed his mind when Churchill threatened to recognise General Giraud as head of the Free French forces in his stead. In June 1943, he and Giraud became Co-Presidents of the French Committee of National Liberation (FCNL), with Giraud remaining in charge of the French Armed Forces. But this situation was not to last long and in November 1943 de Gaulle forced Giraud to surrender his seat in the FCNL so that he, de Gaulle, could become the undisputed single President. The main charge brought against Giraud was that he had left it until the very last minute before informing the FCNL of his plans for a purely French invasion and liberation of Corsica.

Antoine de Saint-Exupéry (1900–44), the celebrated aviator and author, had, after just over two years of exile in Canada and the USA (1940–43), turned up in Algiers in spring 1943, where his pilot friend General René Chambe (1889–1983), who had played a central role in arranging Giraud's daring escape in 1942 and had been helped in turn by Giraud to get to Algeria in January 1943, was now his Information Minister. Chambe was also friendly with Jacques, and in a letter to him of 10 December 1943 he hoped that after the war the two of them might meet again on his property in France and enjoy the good things in life. One of the many hopeful promises that were not fulfilled.[27] He talked of being invited by Jacques to lunch on the balcony in Algiers with Colonel Keswick and how, at present, after Jacques' departure, they are living through '*des heures lourdes*'.

Despite his considerable flying experience, Saint-Exupéry was considered too old at forty-four to be a military pilot and pestered Chambe to use his influence to get him back into the air and operational. His persistence eventually paid off, and a Lieutenant Maurice Guernier in the *Bataillon de Choc* remembered 'St Ex' coming to their training camp after flying reconnaissance missions over Corsica, having taken photographs which were pretty useless because of the altitude at which he had had to fly. He was very depressed by this, because he desperately wanted to be of some use, and on 31 July 1944 he took off from an airfield in Corsica on a reconnaissance mission in a twin-boomed Lockheed P-38 (Lightning), only to crash into the sea off the south coast of France.[28]

Back on Corsica, CESARI was having some difficulty holding back his

Resistance fighters since Giraud, who feared a blood-bath, wanted them to hold their fire until they could be supported by regular French forces. But although the *Bataillon de Choc* was ready for action by August, after the deposition and subsequent arrest of Mussolini as First Marshal of the Empire on 25 July 1943, nothing happened until 3 September 1943, the day when the Allies signed a secret Armistice with the Italians and invaded Italy. There was a further five days delay until 8 September 1943, when news of the Armistice was made public. By then there was no question of waiting any longer for Giraud's reinforcements: the next day the Corsicans erupted onto the streets of Ajaccio and fighting rapidly spread to other towns.

OPERATION VESUVIUS: THE LIBERATION OF CORSICA (9 SEPTEMBER – 4 OCTOBER 1943)

Once the news of the fighting reached Admiral Sir Andrew Cunningham (1883–1963), C-in-C in the Mediterranean from June 1939 to 21 October 1943 (when he became First Sea Lord of the Admiralty), he asked for the two fast French destroyers/light cruisers *Fantasque* and *Terrible*, currently part of the Allied Naval Force at Salerno, to be returned to Algiers (see Couhat, 1971, frontispiece).[29] And on 12 September 1943, 109 men of the *Bataillon de Choc* were embarked on the submarine *Casabianca*, commanded by Captain Jean L'Herminier (1902–53), and taken to Corsica, where they arrived on the following day with orders to establish a bridgehead and secure the airport. The rest of the Bataillon, with Colonel Deleuze, as well as Carlton Stevens Coon (1904–81), Professor of Anthropology at the University of Pennsylvania, who was affiliated to the OSS which involved him in espionage and smuggling arms to the French Resistance in Morocco, arrived at Ajaccio with a small American commando on the 14 September. Coon had also been involved in the training of French youths at MASSINGHAM.

General Henry Martin (1888–1984), whom Giraud had put in charge of Operation Vesuvius (i.e. the liberation of Corsica) and the reconstituted French I Corps in August 1943, left Algeria on the *Fantasque* on 16 September, accompanied by the *Terrible*, and arrived at Ajaccio at 01.00 hours on the following day with orders to establish a bridgehead as soon as possible. He was accompanied by

Captain Négrié and Lieutenant Hage and Lieutenant Sanguinetti (aviation), the British Commandant GILLES (aka de Guélis) with his own Mission consisting of Captains Hodgart[30] and Mills, two wireless operators, and two NCOs. Jacques had been given a carefully constructed alter ego of GILLES or GILLIES by which he appears to have been known by the French in Algiers. Also on board was an OSS agent, Lieutenant Gerry de Piolenc, who may have been part of a team of US commandos of American-Italian origin that had been recruited by Max Corvo (1920–94).[31] It is worth noting that John Kempthorne says his SOE party left Algiers eight days before Jacques and the French contingent.

General Henry Martin

The representative of the Allied C-in-C, General Peake arrived on 19 September with a US Italian commando.

The HQ of the Allied Forces in North Africa had requested OSS to supply a token Allied force to accompany the French, and Major-General William Donovan (1883–1959), the Head of OSS, selected a group of two officers and thirty other ranks, plus a demolitions instructor and one or two other men. This group, accompanied by French reinforcements, left Algiers on French destroyers on 17 September at the same time as Jacques. Very little has been written about their mission, particularly in French accounts, except for brief mentions of the small US commando force.[32]

It is tempting to think that Jacques was using his alias during the crossing for fear of being discovered by the hostile de Gaulle, though in the hot-house of Algiers, he would have found it almost impossible to hide his identity, not least because of his size. His alias does appear in footnotes in *La Libération de la Corse* by Raymond Sereau (1955)[33] and he almost certainly fell foul of de Gaulle because of his connection with General Giraud whom, according to his mother, he admired but who had supposedly initiated the invasion of Corsica by French forces without properly informing de Gaulle.

After landing in Ajaccio, the newly appointed Prefect, M. Luizet, plus General Mollard, the French Military Governor of the island who had designed its formidable defences before its capture by the Italians, and General Martin lost no time in visiting the GOC of the Italian VII Corps during the afternoon of 17 September, while Jacques and his mission joined CESARI in Ajaccio in order to help organise patriots in the area. But on 18 September, Jacques, together with General Gambiez and CESARI, was definitely present at a meeting in Ajaccio that was convened by General Martin in order to plan the deployment of the *Bataillon de Choc* over the coming days (Sereau, 1955, p. 46, n.16). On 19 September, General Peake, the representative of the Allied C-in-C, landed in Ajaccio in earnest of the Allies' interest in the island. On 20 September, Jacques' mission split up and went off into different areas of the island in order to assist the patriots. They had also promised to keep MASSINGHAM informed of their specific local situation and to indicate where arms and ammunition were most needed.

Old postcard of General Giraud (1879–1949) in Corsica

Because the telegram announcing his arrival had been delayed, General Giraud arrived in Corsica unexpectedly by air early in the morning of 21 September, accompanied by Generals Bouscat and Chambe. Another meeting was held in Ajaccio's Hotel Continental between the Prefect and the generals, but Jacques may well have been elsewhere. At 14.00 hours on the same day, a naval convoy consisting of the *Fantasque*, the destroyer *Tempête*, the light cruiser *Jeanne d'Arc* and the destroyer *Alcyon*, swept in, unloaded men and arms, and departed for Algiers two hours later. At which point CESARI, exhausted by his incessant criss-crossing of the island, was suddenly taken ill and had to go to hospital, where Giraud, on 22 September, made him a Chevalier of the Legion d'Honneur. His command of the Corsican irregulars was then assumed by Colonel Clipet from the office of General Ronin, the Head of Giraud's Special Services, who, as a professional soldier, disliked their unprofessional way of waging war and tried to make them fight like regular soldiers rather than make use of their well-developed talent for sabotage and ambush. This change of tactics was not a success and the OSS report mentions the fact that French regular officers tended to deprecate and thus antagonise the leaders of the Maquis.[34] So it was fortunate that General Martin was on hand because he was familiar with mountain warfare, liked and understood the Corsican people, and knew how best to deploy their particular military expertise (Gambiez, p. 173).

On 22 September, Generals Giraud and Martin travelled round the island on a tour of inspection. At Corte, they received General Magli, the Commander of all the Italian forces on Corsica, and they then went south to Levie where they inspected part of the *Bataillon de Choc* and the patriot fighters, and thence to Sartène.

But on 28 September 1943, i.e. even before Corsica was completely free, an advance party of SOE's MISSION BALACLAVA had left Algiers on board the *Serenini*, a 60-ton yawl which the French Navy used as a training vessel, with 15 tons of stores.[35] It first put into Ajaccio, where its Commanding Officer, the quondam polar explorer Major Andrew Croft (1906–98),[36] had orders, dated 27 September, to make contact with Jacques' Mission so that he, via his contact in the French High Command, could facilitate Croft's mission and square things with Generals Peake and Martin. Major Croft was the field officer in charge of naval operations for the Allied Special Forces, and he was tasked with setting up a base in Corsica from which clandestine operations could be launched into occupied Italy and Southern France, using coastal forces and high-speed craft. Croft also had a directive in French from General Ronin, the Head of Giraud's Special Services, to General Martin, saying that Commandant GILLES (i.e. de Guélis) would liaise between Croft and the French Command on Corsica (Richards, 1996, *Secret Flotillas*, pp. 647–51, 654–5) and Andrew Croft's orders in his daughter's possession.

Colonel Noel Andrew Cotton Croft, DSO,OBE (JC)

Croft's orders throw some light on Jacques' work on the island. He appears to have been appointed by the French as Liaison Officer between the French High Command and the various Allied elements that were also on the island. According to Kempthorne's letter, Jacques had an office in Ajaccio but the general impression is that he was moving around the island as it was being liberated. So how do Kempthorne and his two NCOs fit into all this? What were they doing on Corsica and who sent them? Kempthorne claims that he was tasked, firstly, with training the *Bataillon de Choc* in Algiers and, secondly, with persuading the Corsican partisans to give up their weaponry – some hope! Kempthorne made these rather grandiose claims in a long letter he wrote to Leading Seaman Don Miles, (see note 24) who was in a group of SOE personnel with Major Andrew Croft (see note 36) operating out of Bastia, 1943–44. Kempthorne also claims that he had been detailed to introduce Major Croft to the Corsican partisans. But Croft's orders stated explicitly that he was to contact Jacques in order to liaise with the military. So who did send Kempthorne? He says that Jacques was planning operations on behalf of SOE, but that he, Kempthorne, had nothing to do with this aspect

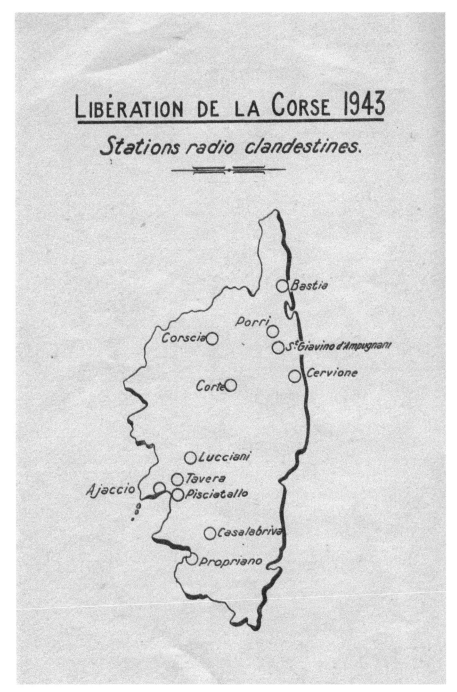

Simple map of Corsica showing clandestine radio stations in 1943

of his role. His account of the aborted parachute jump, however, contradicts various official reports that Jacques was parachuted into Corsica and coupled with General Martin's letter confirming that he went by sea, it may be assumed that this part of his account is accurate.

In a letter of 6 October 1945 from Algiers to Jacques' widow,[37] General Martin said that her husband had often accompanied or preceded him on his forays into the mountains during that brief period when the French were driving the Germans out of the eastern part of the island and into the sea. So it is very possible that Jacques accompanied the two generals to Levie, particularly since there was fierce fighting in this area between 10 and 19 September, with the *Bataillon de Choc* supporting the indigenous guerrillas and, in the north, with some North African troops as well, while they were engaged on the same task. General Martin's letter also states that as soon as the island had been cleared of the enemy, Jacques left to assist in the preparations for the invasion of Europe. So we may conjecture that after 28 September, i.e. the date of Croft's arrival, he followed the advance northwards towards Bastia, which was finally liberated on 4 October. Corsica was the first French Department to gain its freedom, and the operation had been almost entirely French as Giraud had wished.[38]

POSTSCRIPT TO CORSICA

On 5 October 1943, General de Gaulle arrived unannounced at Ajaccio to begin a triumphal progress around the island on the assumption, as he had said in one of his spats with Giraud, that it was he, de Gaulle, whom the Corsicans were waiting to see! Among those waiting to see him was his cousin, the Corsican Resistance leader Henri Maillot (1899–1987). But Jacques had almost certainly left the island by the time of de Gaulle's arrival, for he was definitely back in Algiers by 8 October. He was still there when he received a letter on 17 October 1943 from Chambe. Addressing him as '*cher ami*' ('dear friend'), Chambe enclosed the wording for the citation for Jacques' *Croix de Guerre* with bronze palm-leaves and wondered in what name, exactly, it should be made out. He expected a reply by return, received it, and sent the citation, signed by General Giraud, on the very next day:

Le Major Jacques Paul Vaillant de Guélis MBE Officier Supérieur de l'Armée britannique qui, durant dix mois, a rendu les plus grands services à l'Armée Française d'Afrique, en particulier au moment de la préparation et de l'exécution de l'opération victorieuse de Corse.

A conquis l'estime de tous par son activité intelligente, son caractère franc et énergetique et le magnifique esprit de camaraderie avec lequel il a tenu à prendre part, côte à côte avec les soldats français, aux plus durs combats de la campagne corse. A fait l'admiration de tous ses frères d'armes par sa bravoure et son mépris total du danger.

Cette citation ouvre de droit au port de la Croix de Guerre avec palme, Signé: Giraud

General Gubbins recalled Jacques to Baker Street on 27 October 1943 as de Gaulle had allegedly forbidden any more dealings with him, and SOE's HQ seems also to have believed that as someone who was not a Gaullist, he had become a liability in an outfit that was becoming overwhelmingly pro-de Gaulle. In London, Jacques joined the Low Countries, France and Allied Directorate as assistant to Lieutenant-Colonel J. R. H. Hutchinson (who was on the staff of Mr R. E. Brook for the D-Day planning), and was replaced as head of MASSINGHAM'S 'Country Section' in Algiers by Lieutenant-Commander Brooks Richards who had been involved in SOE naval operations between Gibraltar and Corsica and who had this to say in a letter of 23 March 1996 to Major Everett :

De Guélis was, I must add, a man of outstanding charm, intelligence and courage. He served SOE with distinction, but General de Gaulle bitterly resented the fact that the British Clandestine services (SOE & SIS) worked in France independently as well as in liaison with the Free French BCRA and it was this that led to de Guélis' supercession from a job in North Africa for which he was eminently qualified and which was of increasing importance as plans for an Allied landing took shape.[39]

He added that he was fortunate in inheriting Jacques' cousin, Captain Barbier (Val), as his second-in-command. But apart from some trips to London, Brooks Richards remained in Algiers until the Allied landings in Provence between 15 and 26 August 1944 (OPERATION DRAGOON).

Chambe wrote to Jacques once more, in December 1943, when the latter was back in London, and he recalled them sitting together on the balcony where he was now sitting with Val Barbier.[40] They had promised to visit each other after the war and he, Chambe, was going to show Jacques his dogs and they would admire his trees and appreciate life in freedom. He mentions that they were going through a rough patch in Algiers, no doubt referring to the now bitter hostility between Giraud and de Gaulle who thought, with more than a little justification, that Giraud had not kept him or the FCNL fully informed on his plans for the invasion of Corsica and was horrified that Giraud had not only armed Communist Resistance groups on the island but given the Front National, a political grouping with pronounced Communist sympathies, virtual control there. This hostility resulted in de Gaulle becoming the sole President of the FCNL in November 1943 and leaving Giraud out on a military and political limb when he, de Gaulle, left North Africa on 30 December to take up his new position at SHAEF. De Gaulle's final act in the feud was to force Giraud into retirement in April 1944.

It is unlikely that the nature and scope of Jacques' activities in Corsica will ever now come to light. A prominent appeal in the newspaper *Corse Matin* in September 2008 entitled '*Qui a connu le major Jacques Vaillant de Guélis?*' and also on the A. Bandera museum website in 2008, as well as enquiries among the former members of the Resistance in Corsica did not produce a single response. And yet it was considered appropriate to send him and his mission to Corsica with General Martin, who clearly, judging from his subsequent letters to the family, had as high a regard for him as did Paul Colonna d'Istria. There is a family story that, while on the island, Jacques was held up at gunpoint and who, 'when things got sticky' an old soldier said of him '*C'est un père*' (a letter, written after the war, to Isabelle Barbier from Nancy – probably Hackwood, a family friend). Whatever he did there merited a *Croix de Guerre*, so there it has to remain – a man, larger than life, who has faded into the wild mountains of the region. He was never awarded the *Légion d'Honneur* and de Gaulle's spite also extended to Generals Giraud, Chambe and Martin who were not included in the Order of the Companions of the Liberation which de Gaulle had created. He also went on to re-write the history of the Resistance in France, air-brushing out as much of the Allied involvement as he could, beginning with his speech from the Hotel de Ville in Paris on 25 August 1944, at the liberation of Paris. There was barely any mention of Allied help or involvement. The Liberation was an entirely French affair. Although de Gaulle had good reason for this, his lack of generosity is striking.

But de Gaulle did not get everything his own way. On 26 February 1944, Giraud, perhaps to spite the General, showed his continuing appreciation of Jacques' work on Corsica by awarding him the *Croix de Guerre* with bronze palm-leaves (Hutchins and Sheppard, 2004, p. 86)!

Jacques, who would have been familiar with the products of the *grandes écoles* among his French family and friends, would have been naturally drawn to generals like Giraud, Chambe and Martin who represented the 'old school'. This is evident in the letters they wrote after his death. In his conversation with Pierre Bloch in 1941 he appears less than entusiastic about de Gaulle. By all accounts de Gaulle's behaviour caused infuriation and exasperation throughout the war so it is not surprising that Jacques may not have been an admirer and there is a hint that he may have been indiscreet on the subject. It must be stressed, however, that Jacques left no comments of his own, so this is conjecture. In the next chapter we will see that Jacques took part in an inter-allied mission in France which was under direct EMFFI (*Etat-Major des Forces Françaises de l'Intérieur*) control.

However, attitudes are changing and as the years pass, more and more information is released by governments and valuable facts emerge which will oblige historians to reassess these war years and present events in a different light.

It has to be said, however, that MASSINGHAM and the Corsican story are full of contradictions, mysteries and errors. It would seem that in September 1944 the island was crawling with different groups/missions – mostly unofficial: SOE, OSS, Carleton Coon, American-Italian commandos, Kempthorne. Small wonder that de Gaulle wanted the island's liberation to be a French affair.

Val Barbier

FOOTNOTES

[1] Massingham files – HS7/169 and HS7/170.

[2] Telegram from de Guélis to his cousin Val Barbier confirming the death of their cousin. Eric Duncan and the above mentioned letter from Jocelyn Bethall in note 10 or 11.

[3] General Jean de Lattre de Tassigny was the OC Vichy forces in Tunisia in 1941. In 1942 he returned to mainland France to take over the 16th Division in Montpélier, began to turn it into an anti-German force and was arrested, tried and sentenced to ten years in prison. But he escaped to Algeria and in October 1943 became GOC of the French 1st Army. Later he would play a leading role in the invasions of Corsica and Southern France.

[4] See Macintyre, 2010, pp. 178–97.

[5] Henri Robert d'Orléans (1908–-99), otherwise known as the Comte de Paris.

[6] Dodds-Parker believed Keswick to be a brilliant and sensitive intelligence officer (Dodds-Parker's papers, Magdalen College, Oxford) and *Setting Europe Ablaze* p. 116 – Keswick was resented by certain intelligence circles whose information and judgement had not proved as correct. In Harold Macmillan War Diaries for 1943–45 when he was British Minister Resident in North Africa he refers to a Luncheon with Dodds- Parker 'who runs one of the queer organisations here called SOE', p. 144.

[7] HS7/169: There are so many conflicting stories about the political situation in North Africa at the time of the landings that it is hard to get at the truth. In particular: French versions of events do not necessarily tally with Allied ones. Did Roosevelt envisage treating with the Vichy Government after the war? Was Darlan forewarned about the landings and put in place pre-emptively? What should be done about the hard-line pro-Vichy groups such as the *Corps franc d'Afrique* and the *Chantiers de jeunesse*? Dodds-Parker (1983) believed that most were patriots waiting for a chance to join the Allies (*Setting Europe Ablaze*, pp. 109–17) Bob Maloubier thought it was 'Byzantine'. Churchill, who had a much clearer grasp of the situation than the Americans, was determined to have nothing to do with Vichy but had to defer to Roosevelt for the time being.

[8] *Nageurs de Combat* by Bob Maloubier, p. 18. The gun question never seems to have been satisfactorily solved. Carlton Coon claimed to have given Bonnier one as had SOE and Cordier offered him d'Astier's and other guns have been mooted, so the mystery remains.

[9] De Guélis had a reputation as a *bon viveur* with a very large appetite to match his size. Henry Hyde, an OSS man in Algiers who spoke perfect French, and had become chief of SI France and who got along with him very well, remembered being entertained by him in a plush little Algerian apartment. He remembered his footballer's frame and deep voice. He said that he was a great Epicurean and served better food than the local diplomats and top brass, but that he would never disclose his source of good wines. Anxious to repay him for his hospitality, Hyde found out that de Guélis enjoyed French ballad singers and managed to find him some Edith Piaf records, including *Mon Légionnaire* (Brown, 1982, p. 326). Henry Hyde was an interesting man, American but educated in France and Britain, and a fluent French speaker. There are some errors in his reports such as calling de Guélis John de Guélis or Le Capitaine Jacques but his description of the man is unmistakable..

[10] Violette Szabo, GC, MBE (1921–45†; executed in KZ Ravensbruck on *c.* 5 February 1945), agent Louise. She was captured near Limoges on 10 June 1944, during her second mission to France and her story forms the basis of the feature film *Carve her Name with Pride* (1958).

[11] Pierre Raynaud, field name Alain, operational name Linkman/Porte-Flamabeau, Psuedonymn Robinet. He was subsequently infiltrated into South-east France to work with the highly successful agent Francis Cammaerts (note 5, Ch. 3).

[12] Entry in Buckmaster's diary 5 June 1943. In September he was in London looking for a flat. His wife recuperating at Bisham Abbey (family letter).

[13] See the letter of 17 October 1943 and 10 December 1943 from General Chambe to de Guélis. Letters in author's possession. General Ronin, Giraud's Chef de Services Spéciaux.

[14] Letter of August, 1943.

[15] For informative biographies of prominent members of the Corsican Resistance, Google '*Amis de la Resistance en Corse du sud*'.

[16] See Hodgkinson, Fred Scamaroni in *Operation Sea Urchin & Guy Verstraete*, Réseau Frédérique, 1994.

[17] See Terry Hodgkinson – FREDERICK L*a Mission Oubliée,* pp. 25–30.

[18] *FREDERICK La Mission Oubliée* by Terry Hodgkinson, 2007.

[19] Dedication to Val Barbier on a page of the *Bulletin Corse* comprising a lecture given by Colonna d'Istria in 1947.

[20] This is made clear in the introduction to a lecture given by Paul Colonna d'Istria in *Bulletin Corse*, February 1947.

[21] HS9/780/5. Opened in November 2006 when the author provided the National Archives with his dates of birth and death. Personal file of Paul Colonna d'Istria.

[22] HS9/780/5.

[23] HS9/780/5.

[24] A private letter written by Kempthorne outlining his exploits. Some of his claims and activities do not fit in to the general scheme of things but his account of the aborted parachute drop is probably accurate although lacking an exact date. It is not quite clear what Kempthorne's role in Corsica was to be. John Philip Kempthorne's Personal File HS9/828/5 states that he was a regular soldier in the Royal Scottish Fusiliers.

[25] See letter from the Windsor Archives of 8 February 2007 confirming the King's visit to SOE HQ in Algiers. Brooks Richards in *Secret Flotillas* states in error that the King awarded him the DSO on the spot. The King did meet Colonna d'Istria and was impressed by him. His DSO insignia were sent to the War Office in April, 1944. Val Barbier wrote home at the time from Algiers '… I was looked at by the King!'

[26] As Cesari refused any payment for his mission, the British authorities arranged for him to be given two lengths of cloth with one lining, enough for two suits, and a pair of shoes from the officers' shop. See his own account in *Bulletin Corse* February 1947. Lecture by Paul Colonna d' Istria, *La Libération de la Corse.* pp. 11–38.

[27] Letter in author's possession see note 14.

[28] Although the wreck of Saint-Exupéry's aircraft was discovered in 2000, much mystery surrounds his death (Google Saint-Exupéry).

[29] The two French ships had been refitted at Boston, Mass., in March 1943, and were capable of reaching speeds of over 45 knots.

[30] HS9/724/1 Hodgart 1916–1996 was an STS instructor. Left for Algiers 21 February 1943 and became a paramilitary instructor. His PF states that he went to Corsica with CLISSOLD Mission from September to October which tempts us to assume that this was the name of de Guélis' mission of seven men on board the *Fantasque*.

[31] Max Corvo was a US Army Private who had the idea of recruiting Italian immigrants for the invasion of Sicily and Italy. One of his recruits was Gerry de Piolenc, actually of French extraction, who joined the OSS and spent 1942–45 in Italy. A small US commando did go into Corsica and de Piolenc's presence on the *Fantasque* suggests that it was on board on 16 September. Enquiries about the crew and passengers on the *Fantasque* did not produce any names and such that I have derived are from various sources: the Massingham files, Gambiez, 1973 *et al.* For more information, Google 1942 (Biagio) Max Corvo or see Corvo, 2005.

[32] War Office Report of Strategic Services in the National Archive at College Park, Maryland, USA

[33] Raymond Sereau p. 44 footnote where Général Henri Martin was accompanied by le Major britannique Gilles and others and p. 46 le commandant Gilles took part in a meeting in Ajaccio on 18 September 1943 together with General Martin, Gambiez and Colonna d'Istria. We know

that de Guélis was using his alias because in General Chambe's first letter regarding his citation, he asks him which name he wants used. Letter dated as above in note 13.

[34] Gambiez – p. 173 and Giraud – p. 253.

[35] See ADM 223/481 in the National Archives.

[36] Noel Andrew Cotton Croft 1906-1990. Participated in several Arctic expeditions. In World War II, after serving with a Special Forces Unit behind enemy lines in Tunisia, he was given an independent command in SOE to operate small boats out of Calvi in Corsica on covert missions to French and Italian coasts. In 1944 he was parachuted into SW France to operate behind enemy lines, acmf.org,uk. Crofts' papers in the possession of his daughter Julia Korner now in Corsica.

[37] In the author's possession.

[38] By 1 October, there were 6,500 French officers and men and 11,700 patriot guerrillas on Corsica – plus the American commando of 400 men and all the odd agents, SOE and others, who are rarely mentioned in French accounts of the campaign.

[39] In the author's possession.

[40] Letter from General Chambe to de Guélis of 10 December 1943. In the author's possession.

5

DE GUÉLIS AND THE LIBERATION OF FRANCE (JUNE–SEPTEMBER 1944)

An experienced officer in clandestine work.
Gets on well with the French, but is inclined
to pay too much attention to French politics

Brigadier E. E. Mockler-Ferryman,
January–December 1944
(Comments in de Guélis's personal file) at the National Archives

MISSION TILLEUL: THE BACKGROUND (JUNE 1944)

On 1 June 1944, hundreds of stand-by messages went out from the BBC, followed, on 5 June, by action messages at 09.15 hours on French radio, by which time the Allied invasion fleet was well on its way to France. On receiving their action messages, the SOE circuits were activated and nearly a thousand planned disruptions of the French railway system occurred. In the Indre Department alone, thanks to the networks described in Chapter 3, about 800 disruptions of the railway system would occur during June 1944.

The main line from Paris to Toulouse ran through Châteauroux and Limoges, and it was vital to prevent German troops from leaving the apparent safety of the South of France and moving northwards by rail to reinforce the German troops who were fighting in Normandy (Vickers, 1999).[1] On the day after the Normandy landings, an élite *Waffen-SS* Armoured Division known as *Das Reich*, which had already gained a reputation for utter ruthlessness on the Eastern Front and was now awaiting supplies and reinforcements at Toulouse, was ordered north to reinforce the Normandy front. It expected to reach Normandy in three days, but pushed northwards very slowly and it took fifteen, by which time it was too late to push the Allies off the invasion beaches. The delay was brought about partly by the activities of the Maquis with SOE help, who harassed the Germans and blew up key features like bridges across rivers and partly by sabotage work on the part of French *cheminots* (who disabled rolling stock capable of carrying heavy tanks. The Germans' frustration grew until matters came to a head on 9 June, when the Limousin Maquis captured *Sturmbannführer* Helmut Kämpfe (1909–44), a highly decorated German officer who commanded the 4th SS *Panzergrenadier* Regiment, part of *Das Reich. Sturmbannführer* Adolf Diekmann, who commanded the 1st Battalion of Kämpfe's Regiment, allegedly received information from the local French *Milice* that the Maquis had captured an SS officer – who was presumed to be Kämpfe – and intended to burn him alive on 10 June in the village of Oradour-sur-Vayres. But Diekmann confused that village with the similarly-named village of Oradour-sur-Glane and on 10 June arrived at the latter village with a company of his men. On his orders, they massacred 642 of its inhabitants in a particularly brutal way – partly in retaliation for the partisan activity and partly in retaliation for the kidnapping. Only a handful of villagers survived. So on the orders of Colonel Georges Guingouin (1913–2005), the senior partisan leader in the Limousin who had been active there since 1940 and who would become Mayor of Limoges from 1945 to 1947, Kämpfe was executed on the same day and his body burnt. It was during the SS sweeps to find Kämpfe that the SOE agent Violette Szabo (Louise) fell foul of an unexpected road block and was arrested.

Although the long hoped-for French national uprising was finally in progress, it gave de Gaulle, who was in Algiers until about 4/5 June, yet another reason for being furious. Churchill did not tell him about the landings until they were actually underway and worsened things by asking to borrow French troops who were already en route for France. De Gaulle could hardly refuse the request, but the meeting was a stormy one, and, according to General Alan Brooke, occasioned 'a long Cabinet at which we were explained how troublesome de Gaulle was being now that he was fetched back from Algiers! He is now refusing to broadcast unless Eisenhower alters the wording of his own broadcast!! I knew he would be a pest and recommended strongly that he should be left in Africa, but Anthony Eden would insist on bringing him over!' (*op. cit* 2001, p. 554).

By the end of June, Operation OVERLORD had landed nearly 660,000

Allied troops in France. The Allied landings in the South of France began on 15 August, six weeks after D-Day (*Jour-J* in French), and were known as Operation DRAGOON. On the very first day of this neglected operation alone, 11,000 vehicles and 94,000 troops, mainly American and French, landed by sea and air on France's Mediterranean coast between Cavalaire-sur-Mer to the west and Saint-Raphaël to the east. The Allies had learnt major lessons from earlier landings, most of the German troops were second and third-line, resistance was slight, the terrain was not like the deadly *bocage* in Normandy, and casualties on the first day were, as a result, miraculously low (95 killed and 385 wounded).[2] Moreover, the invasion force rapidly secured the ports of Marseille and Toulon, meaning that it was not plagued by the supply problems which had so hampered their comrades in Normandy and beyond, and the Franco-American Army was able to advance rapidly up the Rhône Valley and liberate Lyon on 2 September. The American 7th Army under General Alexander M. Patch (1889–1945) numbered some three divisions, with the majority of the force – 260,000 men, i.e. eight divisions and a brigade – belonging to the French Army B (renamed the First Army from 25 September 1944), commanded by General Jean de Lattre de Tassigny (1889–1952). Most of the French soldiers were colonial troops from Algeria, Morocco and Senegal, but Lattre de Tassigny's force also included the 1st *Régiment de Choc*, an expanded version of the *Bataillon de Choc* that had been formed at Algiers in the previous year with SOE's help. Somewhere among this mass of troops was Jacques' cousin Captain G. 'Val' Barbier.

MISSION TILLEUL: PLANNING SPRING 1944

Months before D-Day, SOE's planning for the missions to be sent into France was well underway. Originally Mission TILLEUL was to be called TRAPPER but the name was officially changed by 16 June, and Jacques was involved from the start.

Jacques had been in Brussels since December 1943 with the Low Countries, France and Allied French Directorate and in April 1944 had attended a reception committee course at Howbury Hall, Waterend, Buckinghamshire (code name STS40) to study Eureka-Rebecca (a short range radio navigation system in two parts. Rebecca being an airborne transeiver and antennae and Eureka a ground-based transponder). He was reported to be enthusiastic about it.

Immediately after D-Day the EMFFI (*Etat-Major des Forces Francaises de l'Intérieur*) was formed to take over both RF section and SOE's F section and direct all resistance in France. The plan was to drop eighty-three three-man JEDBURGH teams made up of French and other Allied personnel into France during the ten weeks after D-Day. Besides these, the Allied back-up included several larger inter-allied missions, one of which was to be TILLEUL. These missions, to be under direct EMFFI control, were to co-ordinate the activities of the Resistance and when needed arrange supply drops.

So in April, Jacques (as DR/M1) was writing asking for various people to be included in his mission. At this point there is a rare opportunity to hear Jacques' voice. It is apparent that Jacques had a major say in the members of what was to be an inter-allied team of seven members. He wanted Teddy Bisset and André Simon with him, both of whom he had known since the early days of the war. Indeed he had attended Teddy Bisset's wedding and André Simon had accompanied him on his escape over the Pyrenees. Others had doubts about André Simon but in the end he prevailed, accepting various provisos from above. It also becomes clear that he had met Jean Lannou in Algiers and wanted him too. So Lannou was to bring quartzes, codes and plans with him from Algiers. Jacques met his co-commander Thomas in May and waited for James Edgar and Major Mackenzie to join the Mission.

Jacques was also tasked with organising supplies and clothing for his team. So he emerges as a good organiser who used his powers of persuasion and probably charm to get his own way.

During planning in May, Jacques mentions being away and a family letter confirms that he had leave at this time. His mother remarked that they would probably not see him for a while.
(*Vincennes, GR 28 P 3 58 SHD*) *Family letter*

Planning completed, the Mission comprised:
Major Jacques Vaillant de Guélis (MANOMÈTRE); 1907–1945
Commandant Thomas (MINIMUM) – French, joint leader of the mission (FFC), representative of the RF (Gaullist) Section of SOE and now revealed as Louis Monguilan; 1902–1982

Major Ian Mackenzie (THERMOMÈTRE) – Surgeon in the RAMC; 1910–

Flight Lieutenant André Simon (DIASTIQUE) – Expert in selecting dropping grounds and parachute receptions (see note 18); 1916–1978

Captain Edward George Alfred Bisset (ADJACENT) – Expert in Arms and explosives; 1915–1944

Sergeant James Edgar (CRÉTOIS) – W/T operator (English); 1905–

Matelot-Radio Jean Georges Lannou (TOSCAN) – W/T operator (French; FFC). 1918–2001

Before TILLEUL's departure, the team was briefed by EMFFI and SOE officers and their destination was to be the densely wooded Department called the Corrèze, 50 miles SE of Limoges, whose major town was Tulle. Their orders in the first place were to head for the Plateau de Millevaches, a relatively unpopulated area of the Massif Central which cuts across the borders of the Creuze and Haute-Vienne Departments as well as those of the Corrèze.

MISSION TILLEUL: THE JUMP-OFF (JULY/AUGUST 1944)

Operation STATIONER127 left RAF Harrington on the night of 7/8 July 1944 in two specially modified, four-engined B-24 Liberator Bombers, each with a crew of eight, and captained by Captains Choper and Driscoll.[3]

Although the Mission was split between the two aircraft, one piloted by Driscoll with three 'Joes' in the one and the other piloted by Choper with four 'Joes', James Edgar only remembered Teddy Bisset being in his Liberator.

The two of them had started out in the Intelligence Corps as field security policemen and had trained together at Wanborough Manor, Guildford, Ringway and Arisaig – but not at Beaulieu. James Edgar had also met Jean Lannou in London, having shared accommodation with him prior to the Mission. Internal security was so tight that Edgar, presumably because he was not an officer, only discovered their destination by asking Bisset: he didn't even know that they had left from Harrington Airfield. He was worried they might have to escape via the Pyrenees. In fact, their destination was near Limoges.

André Simon reported that they were cold during the flight and that, because the teams had been dispatched in a poor, hesitant manner, they had landed quite

Chopper Crew Spring/Summer 1944 (801st/492nd Bombardment Group Association)

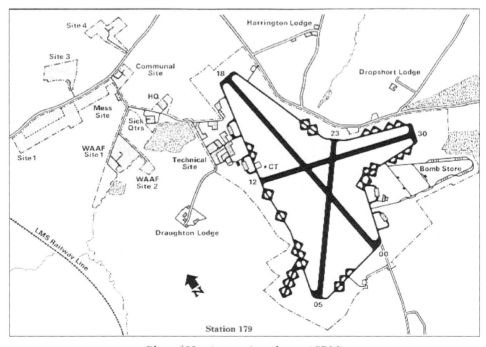

Plan of Harrington Aerodrome (CBM)

far apart.[4] Their reception had been organised by SALESMAN: Phillippe Liewer (Major STAUNTON or HAMLET) and his deputy on landing ground Orange, Bob Maloubier (PACO), was also at the landing ground with Marc Grelon and was quite amazed to see his old Algerian acquaintance, Jacques, among the new arrivals. The teams were gradually located and brought to the meeting point at Le Clos, a long stretch of open ground flanked by trees that is about two miles north of Mont Gargan, a 2,200ft high peak, where, on one night alone in July/ August 1944, 300 four-engined B-17 Flying Fortresses would drop supplies and reinforcements.

After the mission's arrival on 8 July, accounts of its deeds become sketchy. Teddy Bisset had kept its official War Diary, but after he was accidentally shot in

The Liberator

Vichy on 24 September 1944, the Diary was not continued and the original was not found among his effects, and Jacques composed his report from memory. According to Jacques, Commandant Thomas kept complete records of his own – but these have either been destroyed or are waiting, like so much about the once elusive Thomas now revealed as Louis Monguilan, to be studied as Thomas/ Monguilan's details have recently been released by the French military archives.

It has, thanks to the meticulous research of Mme Dominique Seaux, that we now have a timetable of events which include German movements, the vagaries of Mackenzie's hospital, Mission TILLEUL's movements and in addition information on Jedburg James and Captain Wauthier's commandos. We do know that on the evening of its arrival, the mission needed to walk a couple of miles northwards to the village of Sussac, now, sadly, depopulated but a thriving community in 1944, where they had supper and were found lodgings and were able to meet a number of Resistance chiefs from the Haute-Vienne. Mackenzie immediately had a meeting with the officer in charge of FTP medical services in Haute Vienne. There was a lack of medical equipment and Mackenzie called London to arrange a drop of the supplies he had prepared before he left. He made contact with Jean Gorodiche (CURVILIGNE) who had been sent to London by the BCRA to organise medical services in the R5 sector.

Rather to the surprise of the young James Edgar, several photographs of the group were taken, and he wondered why some of the mission's members were in shorts. It was in this village that Mme Ribéras had sheltered Violette Szabo in June during her fateful second mission to France and Maloubier speculated that Jacques may well have stayed in the same house. Mme Riberas was acting

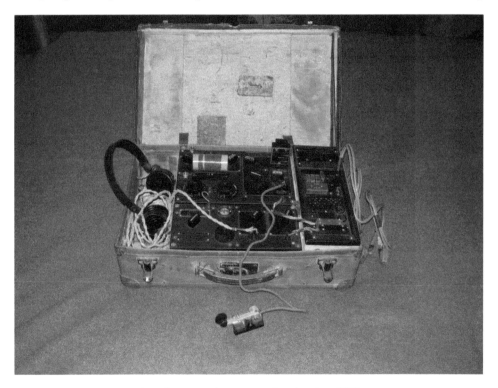

A radio transmitter as used at the time (BB)

Daylight Parachute drop at le Clos, Sussac, 14 July 1944 (BB)

as temporary chief in the absence of her husband who was a POW in Germany.

After a few days in Sussac, on 14 July an armed convoy escorted the mission due east into the Corrèze where, according to Simon, their first HQ was a farm a few miles south-west of Bugeat. Jacques reported that their trip was a comparatively long one, across two national roads and a good number of secondary roads. Simon then set about surveying the district in order to identify the best landing-grounds and named the first of these 'LOUP' ('wolf'). But at one point Commandant Thomas ordered him to stay in their camp because there were Germans at Bugeat and Meymac, twelve or so miles to the south-east.[5]

The mission soon realised that resistance in the Corrèze was far stronger and better organised than they had been led to believe in London. To a considerable extent this was due to the wild and wooded nature of the terrain, with its winding lanes and few good roads, and it must have been increasingly difficult for the Germans, with their eyes elsewhere because of the invasions, to keep even a small fraction of it under surveillance without running the risk of ambushes. But the terrain worked to TILLEUL's advantage for it permitted the mission to come and go pretty well as and when it pleased over a very wide area. So Jacques and Thomas had talks with the various local leaders, all of whom wanted arms urgently and had something to say about the failings of other groups. Very wisely,

Jacques kept out of the politics and left it to Thomas to point out that General Marie-Pierre Koenig (1898–1970), the Commander-in-Chief of the FFI (*Forces Françaises de l'Intérieur*) since D-Day, wished all resisters to consider themselves simply as patriots who were fighting a common enemy as part of a larger force.[6] Lieutenant René Pin, the liaison officer of the Corrèze FFI, had been sent into the Haute Vienne on 11 July 1944 to guide Tilleul's two co-leaders to Lamazière-Basse, seven miles south of the town of Egletons, to meet Léon Lanot (LOUIS) of the FTP (*Franc-Tireurs et Partisans Français*), Lieut Colonel Louis Godefroy, (RIVIÈRE) (1911–18), the then Communist Chief of the Northern Corrèze.[7] On the following day, 12 July, Thomas and Jacques met three FTP representatives, including Joseph Fertig (HANNIBAL) and on the same day Commandant Duret (JEAN CRAPLET) of the AS in Haute Corrèze. Jacques praised René Pin for his assistance and for simultaneously commanding his own company of FFI troops, and although he does not mention Georges Guingouin, the great Communist resistance leader, it is probable that he met him, too.

On either 12 July or 13th Jacques inspected the dam at Marèges, which was important for electricity supplies, and other structures in the Neuvic region.

The Marèges dam (DS2)

The mission was probably based in Sussac until 14 July, when, with René Pin as their guide, its members set about finding themselves an HQ. Marcy, the first village that the mission had singled out for that purpose, had been burnt to the ground by the Germans, so they eventually settled on the house of a local farmer, Justin Sauviat, at Chadebech, a mile to the east of the large village of Bonnefond and some ten miles to the north of Egletons, while the owner was living in another house nearby. Jacques subsequently reported that Sauviat and his wife Micheline looked after the mission for the best part of a month – apart from a week which they spent in the woods. The late Madame Sauviat, (d. December 2013) who still lived (2006) in the same house, told the author that she regarded it as her duty to look after the mission as well as other resisters in the area, and her speciality was, apparently, giant omelettes topped with cheese. Dr Mackenzie, whose medical

Group in front of Butcher's shop. Sussac, July/August, 1944
Back row from left: Bob Maloubier, 2 resistance members, André Simon, Teddy Bisset and Sergeant James Edgar.
Front row from left: Lannou 'radio' for Commandant Thomas, Major Staunton, Jacques de Guélis, a member of the resistance, Comm. Thomas with pipe, Dr. Mackenzie and Marcel la Couture.

work took him further afield, would return to the Sauviat house whenever he could, she said in order to rest up.[8]

Once the HQ was established and in the absence of clear instructions from London, the various members of the mission set about organising themselves. On the day of their arrival, James Edgar had sent his first message to London to say they had landed safely, with no injuries. But London's only reply had been QRU: 'nothing for you', and according to Jacques' report, no further reply from London came until 20 July.[9]

Bob Maloubier with the author, 2006 (GI)

Moreover, promises of arms were made by TILLEUL to various Resistance groups, but Jacques subsequently reported that the first dozen telegrams sent by the mission's two wireless operators Edgar (CRETOIS) and Lannou (TOSCAN) had not been answered – which put them in a difficult position with the local Resistance chiefs. On 18 July Jacques cabled London to ask for an explanation. According to Edgar, he later encountered the code-maker Leo Marks (1920–

2001; see Marks, 1999) who, on seeing him, said: 'Oh my God, Edgar, all your messages went into the waste paper unread. How they got there I do not know!'[10]

In 2016, James Edgar now in his nineties got his answer among the papers related to the planning of the Mission. There had been a mix-up in London between F and RF sections and Edgar/CRETOIS' messages were unanswered by F section hence Leo Marks comments.

Nevertheless, the delay began to annoy Jacques, who wondered 'what the bloody hell are we supposed to do here?' Edgar decided that he would spend the time by brushing up Jacques' and Bisset's command of morse code. Jacques also spent time smoothing things over with local Resistance chiefs: he would then report back to Thomas and Colonel Maurice Rousselier (1914–58) (code name RIVIER) – then the military Chief of RF (the Gaullist SOE) who is sometimes confused with Lieutenant-Colonel Louis Godefroy, one of whose code names was RIVIÈRE. On 16 August, Jacques finally met Eugène Déchelette (code names ELLIPSE, CHASSEIGNE) (1906–73), who had been on de Gaulle's Staff in London since 1941 and parachuted into France on 29 January 1944 as the official *Délégué Militaire Régional* (DMR), i.e. the person responsible for co-

James Edgar outside the épicerie, Sussac (JE)

ordinating the work of and distributing supplies and money to the Resistance groups in the Limousin Region (R5) until September 1944. On one occasion, when Jacques was at HERVÉ'S (René Vaujour, AS chief) camp near Argentat he saw the bodies of five *maquisards* who had been wounded during a skirmish and then finished off by the Germans. Meanwhile, Teddy Bisset, the weapons expert, began training regular French soldiers in the use of the British spring-loaded PIAT (Projectile, Infantry, Anti-Tank) gun and the rocket-propelled American bazooka, and even took part in some of their operations. These regular soldiers were already properly trained in the use of machine-guns and were disciplined, in contrast to many of the *maquisards* who were just youngsters and had fled into the *Maquis* to evade STO (forced labour in Germany). Bisset had also been with the BEF in 1940 in France and had been assigned from Field Security to act as secretary to Captain Whatmore, at GHQ Liaison at the Bureau de Centralisation de Renseignement in Lille.

André Simon, successfully established his landing grounds north of the RN89 between Ussel and Tulle which he named LOUP, LAPIN, CHAMEAU and VACHE, all suitable for night landings and COCHON suitable for daytime, all with their designated letters. He now posed a more difficult problem as he had good reasons for wanting to move south, having set up his circuits in the north of the Corrèze. He also wanted to take James Edgar with him and, with his help, establish an HQ just outside Clergoux, 12 miles due east of Tulle on the D978 and some six miles south of the RN89 (now the D1089). This road, whose importance has been superseded by a modern motorway, cut diagonally through the Corrèze from the north-east to the south-west and connected Clermont-Ferrand in the east with Tulle in the centre and Bordeaux on the east coast. Consequently, it was a key artery for German troops who were trying to reach Normandy from the east and south-east and for Allied troops who were trying to stop them. But before letting Simon go, Thomas wanted to secure the supplies that were needed in the north, before allowing him to have receptions in the south, and there was also a disagreement with Jacques, which ended in a compromise, because this change of plan made things awkward for Simon as he was accused by HERVÉ and others of favouring the FTP. Supplying the north involved a total of six drops in all, and the supplies had to be moved mainly by bullock cart because of the nature of the terrain. (July 30/31 six containers on VACHE and the next night, medical supplies on LAPIN.)

Meanwhile, Major Mackenzie, who had worked with Tito's partisans in Yugoslavia, and was, therefore, no stranger to the dangerous clandestine work, was organising medical facilities. He established field hospitals in various places but often had to move on hurriedly if the Germans came too close. He established good relations with the French medical workers of the region and on the 3 August he attempted set up a hospital at Près-longs (St-Yrieix) but the arrival of the Germans at Egletons cut him off from Jacques. Jeanine Nussbaumer and René Ravaine had been designated to treat the casualties and sick of Egletons. Jeanine Nussbaumer (later Madame Ravaine), was interviewed by some third-year pupils at the Jean-Yves Soulier Collège de Corrèze. (*Août 44: Souvenirs d'une infirmière*) and remembered her experiences. Given the importance of the RN89, it was inevitable that the town of Egletons, which sits astride it, should become a flash-point. So on about 3 August, Mme Nussbaumer was told to go there in her capacity as nurse and care for the people who had been wounded in the fighting which had started there. She was, however, unable to get into the town because the *École Nationale Professionelle* had been taken over by 300 Germans who, like the Panzer Division *Das Reich* in June, were reconnoitring the area in an attempt to find a way northwards into Normandy. On 4 August she met up with Mackenzie, however, setting up a first-aid post in an empty building in the middle of fields near St-Yrieix-le-Déjalat proved impossible so they were obliged to decamp to La Virolle where they were to remain till about 14 August when they were back in St.Yriex at the Maison Taguet and the school. During the next few days they were visited by a chemist and a student chemist, Tony Chabrerie.

On 5 August, Simon[11] eventually got his way and took Edgar to the *Hôtel 'Beau Site'* at St Pardoux-la-Croisille, two miles south of Clergoux. Owned by the Tourette family, the hotel, which is still a hotel today, had been used by Parisians for summer breaks and so was empty at the time. The landing grounds he established in this region were named TAUREAU, ECUREUIL and VEAU for day drops and CHAT for night time. So Edgar, whose role was vital, became the hotel's sole, clandestine occupant and transmitted such messages from there as he received from Simon and Jacques. By looking to the north-east, he could

Hôtel Beau Site (JE)

watch the bombing of Egletons, some 12 miles away, but he also had time to befriend the Tourette's son Jacques and go swimming with him.[12]

A meeting was held at Thalamy on 10 August with Thomas, Jacques, Simon and several delegates including CURVILIGNE, BARON and SÉCATEUR to wait for the announcement of arrivals there. The landing ground at Thalamy, named COCARDE, figures in the messages to and from TOSCAN and CRETOIS through most of August 1944 and into September but no arrivals ever landed. There is a photo in *L'Armée Secrète en Haute-Corrèze* by Le Moigne and Barbanceys 1979, taken at Thalamy, a good thirty miles to the east-north-east of Chadebec, where André Simon (third from the left in RAF uniform) had apparently asked AS (*Armée Secrète*) for an old French military auxiliary ground to be made ready in time for important persons to land on 10 August. According to Simon's report (HS6/587) heavy rain twice played a part rendering the ground unsuitable and the Germans had dug trenches across the runway to render it useless.

At Chadebec, LANNOU, Mission TILLEUL'S other radio operator heard the 'message personnel' '*N'aimez-vous pas les mandarines*', warning reception committees of parachute landings in their area and on the night of 10/11

Thalamy airport (DS2)

August, two four-engined Short Stirling aircraft of 190 Squadron, flying from RAF Fairford in Gloucestershire and piloted by Pilot Officer Sellars and Flight-Sergeant Coesholt, dropped some twenty-six reinforcements plus equipment, led by Captain Claude Wauthier. The drop took place at Fonfreyde and was receptioned by André Simon. Wauthier and his commandos were installed in a farm, lost in the woods, near Chadebec, under the protection of the AS, and Mme Nussbaumer, who remembers the sky as being 'starry with white parachutists', went to meet it with Mackenzie and was given cigarettes and that evening's edition of the London newspapers.[13] Dropped at the same time was JEDBURGH JAMES, a three man team consisting of John K. Singlaub (MISSISSIPPI), Jacques Lebel de Penguilly (MICHIGAN) and Anthony Denneau (MASSACHUSETTS). Simon was present later that day at a meeting between HUBERT at their hiding place when HUBERT explained to the JEDBURGHS his need for arms and Denneau sent a message that afternoon requesting arms for HUBERT (Léonard

WEL 8996 JTB
SERIAL NO A 3482   PRIORITY P + O SECTION FIGHTING FRANCE 63
TO CRETOIS   VIA TRAPPER VOIE DIRECTE
PREFIX F A W OTP   10TH AUGUST 44   ORIG NO 15

POUR DIASTIQUE STOP SUJET TERRAIN COCARDE JE DIS COCARDE TOP
HOMOLOGATION RETARDEE TOP AIR MINISTRY VEUT SAVOIR SI TRANCHEES
ONT ETE BOUCHEES AVEC PIERRES ET NON AVEC TERRE ET BIEN DAMEES
DE FACON AUE L'APPAREIL NE S'ENFONCE PAS EN PASSANT SUR
TRANCHEES TOP NOTRE UN CINQ DU UN ZERO AUOT TOP GOOD NIGHT

THI 1760 GMT
TP AT 0137 GMT 11TH AUGUST 44 DC
OK
O. RLSE 0138 GMT
QSL NC

FQD
QWZEEWWS62YWBOYV JTL

SRL NR A 1326/25   FROM: CRETOIS VIA TRAPPER
TOR 0821 GMT   23RD AUGUST 44
PREFIX: D G C   SPECIAL CHECK PRESENT
WATERPROOF   1539

? RAILWAY NINE OF TWENTY TWO FROM MANOMETRE TOG TELL MY WII
HHR CABLE RECVD AND I AM MOST WELL TOP MF LOVE TO MY MOTHER

LETTERS 95
   TP 1019/22 GMT   23RD AUGUST 44   DM++++
OK

OK RLSE 1020
QSL   EP

2 Radio messages from TILLEUL – SHD GR 28 P3 58 Vincennes

Hounau – Corps Franc, Tulle) and the SAS. Wauthier demanded arms too to carry out his mission. Apparently Wauthier caused some hilarity on his arrival by declaring that he had come to the Corrèze to blow up the railways. The trains had not been running for quite some time! There was a serious disagreement between TILLEUL and Wauthier as revealed in the radio messages of TOSCAN ; it seems Wauthier asked London to allow him to take over military command and command of TILLEUL. This was badly received by TILLEUL, ELLIPSE, the DMR and London and brought a sharp rebuke from London (25 August for Wauthier via TOSCAN) and he was reminded that his commandos were at the disposition of TILLEUL. It was proposed that his group be sent to Toulouse out of the way, however, they were eventually sent into the Creuse instead!

On 12 August, Mission TILLEUL received news that the FTP were planning to mount a full-scale attack on the holed-up Germans in the *École Nationale* and both Thomas and Jacques who thought an attack was premature, tried to dissuade ANTOINE, but without success. It was agreed, however, that Thomas, Jacques and one of the FTP officers commanded by Lieutenant-Colonel Roger Lecherbonnier (ANTOINE), who had recently taken over as FTP Commander for the northern Corrèze, should try to negotiate a surrender with the German Commander. So that evening, under cover of a white flag, they sent in a mediator – but the Germans refused to negotiate and on the morning of 14 August the School was attacked – unsuccessfully – and a siege began at which Thomas, Jacques and Bisset were sporadically present. During the siege, which lasted until 22 August, the Germans attacked the French some eighteen to twenty times using bombers and fighters which continued to dive on the besiegers long after they had used up all their bombs and ammunition. Bisset (ADJACENT) went from group to group in the front line, encouraging them; London was asked to send in Mosquito aircraft to bomb the School – which it did on 19 August; René Pin's men got close enough to the building to set fire to the roof and top storey with PIAT bombs. Eventually the Germans broke out, retreated south-westwards towards Tulle, and finally pulled out of the Corrèze, while being harried and ambushed all the way.

Meanwhile Wauthier contacted TILLEUL at the Hotel Fonfreyde at Egletons and they went to Bonnefond to wait for an important parachute drop while

ICI

DU 14 AU 18 AOUT 1944
LES UNITES DES FORCES
FRANCAISES DE L' INTERIEUR
LES PARAS DES FORCES FRANCAISES
LIBRES
LA ROYAL AIR FORCE
LIVRERENT COMBAT A UN BATAILLON
DU 194 EME REGIMENT DE LA WEHRMACHT
HARCELE ET ENCERCLE DEPUIS LE 4 AOUT
MALGRE LE SOUTIEN DE L' AVIATION
ALLEMANDE

EN HOMMAGE A LA POPULATION D'EGLETONS
A LA MEMOIRE DES COMBATTANTS
DE LA LIBERTE

Top: Plaque at school entrance

Bottom: Plaque at St.Yrieux

En ce lieu du 15 au 18 Août 1944
a été installé un hôpital
de campagne dans lequel
le major anglais Jan MACKENZIE
assisté du médecin René RAVAINE et
de l'infirmière Jeanine NUSSBAUMER
a soigné et opéré les combattants
de la résistance blessés
lors des combats d'EGLETONS

Lebel and Singlaub left on a reconnaissance survey of the region and also chose a landing ground for the SAS. CORIOLAN (Saar-Demichel Franz) the regional information officer visited and told them that Antoine's men had moved towards Egletons in the night. The three Jedburghs with ten of HUBERT'S men set off on foot for the town. Several meetings between the groups and Wauthier with Singlaub's help fired mortars at the school

While all this was going on at Egletons, Commandant DURET (Jean Craplet, Commandant AS for la Haute Corrèze) at Ussel, fifteen miles away to the north-east, was asking urgently for more arms and ammunition since the Resistance had encircled the garrison there too, also in a local school. Thomas collected some bren guns and ammunition and set off with Jacques. But as they approached Ussel they saw a pall of smoke hanging over it. The French had acquired a German machine-gun and were firing round after round of incendiary bullets at exactly the same spot: this eventually caused the school to catch fire and the garrison came out and surrendered on 17 August.

The school at Egletons with bullet marks

Once the fighting had begun in earnest in Egletons on 14 August, Mackenzie, his hospital now established at near-by St-Yrieix-le-Déjalat, began to receive the wounded and Jacques was told by his colleagues that Mackenzie himself had carried out some remarkable operations At first, his staff consisted of three people, with Mackenzie and Dr René Ravaine doing the operations and Mlle Nussbaumer preparing the patients. Later, Tony Chabrerie came to assist, bringing with him his sister Georgette Chabrerie (d. May 2016) who had just finished training as a nurse, and several more people turned up to lend a hand. By 17 August, the number of wounded had decreased and on 18 August the team upped sticks and went to the school-house in the village of Sarran, seven miles to the west, where they received a few more wounded during the course of the day. The school-house was empty in the summer except for an English teacher who was trapped by the war, and she made tea and got her visitors to repeat some rudiments of the language. Mackenzie operated on Lucien Duval at Sarran on 20 August and Joseph Molinier on the 21st (he did not survive). Lebel and Singlaub spent ten days instructing ANTOINE and HUBERT'S men and Thomas and Jacques visited Ussel on the 17th and promised the FFI a drop of munitions which never materialised. On his return, Jacques visited Mackenzie while Bisset was in the thick of the fighting. During the night, Mackenzie was woken up by a German relief column en route to Egletons that passed within 200 yards of them. So he woke the others, and the group, using small footpaths, made its way north-westwards towards le Salvaneix and the Château de Bity, a mile or so away.

On 20 August the Germans finally left Egletons, and reached Ussel after several ambushes on 21st.

In his mission report Edgar told how after the bombing of the school at Egletons when three remaining Germans and one other had been killed, he was confronted by a French father who told him that his eighteen-year-old son had been in the building during the bombardment. He also remembered an American airman who stayed with TILLEUL at Chadebec until he was flown back to the UK.

THE LIBERATION AND AFTER

On 10 September, Mission Tilleul had gathered in the Chateau de Sainte-

James Edgar (JE)

Fortunade, before leaving, some for Vichy, some for home while one, Bisset, was accidentally shot in Vichy.

By this time, the Liberation was spreading rapidly all over the region. Brive-la-Gaillarde was liberated on 15 August, Tulle, for the second time, on 16 August, Ussel on 17 August, Limoges on 21 August, the Corrèze as a whole on 22 August, Paris on 25 August and Vichy on 26 August when the Germans finally left. Bob Maloubier remembered that when it was necessary to address villagers, as in the little town of Eymoutiers in the Haute-Vienne, Jacques' French was so perfect that nobody would have believed that he was in the English Army. So André Simon was detailed to speak instead because his French accent was too awful for words and thus highly authentic. Maloubier, together with Georges Guingouin, also witnessed the German surrender on the steps of the Hôtel de la Paix in Limoges and Maloubier recalled that Jacques and other agents stayed there in what had been the City's Gestapo HQ and James Edgar confirmed this.

By then, TILLEUL's mission had done its work. When we were driving towards

The house belonging to M.and Mme Sauviat at Chadebec, used as Tilleul HQ (JW)

Sussac with Bob Maloubier in 2006, he announced, as we were crossing a bridge over the River Briance at St Germain des Belles, that he had blown it up in 1944. In fact he had spent several days blowing things up and was then wounded for the second time on 4 September, near Mézières (Indre), while trying to take several German prisoners single-handed.

After the mission was terminated in late August, it moved its HQ to Sainte Fortunade, three miles due south of Tulle having given the Ussel FFI some ammunition from an old drop. Its members made at least one trip to Limoges to see Eugène Déchelette (ELLIPSE) and obtain instructions from him in his capacity as the DMR. He asked the mission to remain and help organise the FFI in case there was further need of them, but perhaps those trying to re-establish order also thought that the mission's presence would inhibit the more extreme elements from abusing their newly-won power.

In early September, however, both RIVIER and ELLIPSE asked Jacques and

Group at St. Fortunade (GC)
From the left: The 'radio' M.Touloumier (or Couloumier), unknown, Paulette Nouaille,
Jacques, Dr. Mackenzie, Georgette Chabrerie and the chauffeur.

other members of TILLEUL if they would join a mobile FFI column under
Colonel Joly which was hoping to join the troops of General Lattre de Tassigny
over in the east of France. The idea was that their experience might enable them
to discover more suitable landing grounds and that they could also act as liaison
officers when they met American troops. Jacques was delighted and took Simon
with him, leaving other members of the Mission to join them later. So the two men
left Limoges on 14 September in order to identify suitable landing grounds, and
according to Simon they went as far as Dijon in one direction and Bordeaux in the
other. But when their radio messages were cut off without warning, they returned
to Limoges for more instructions. Here they were advised to wait a few days and
then go to Paris if no contact had been made with London. Meanwhile, Thomas,
Edgar and Bisset had been ordered back to London and Staunton(Lieuwer) left

on 16 September, but whereas Thomas and Edgar left by air, Bisset decided to make his own way back overland.

On 16 September 1944 Jacques was awarded his third Croix de Guerre, this time with a silver star. According to the citation by Colonel Rousselier (RIVIER), this presentation, involving other Allied personnel, took place in Limoges on the

Teddy Bisset (WB)

17 September. A ceremony clearly did take place then, for photographs and a documentary film still survive. On page 220 of *Visages de la Resistance 1940– 1944*, edited by Pascal Plas there is a list of awards to Allied officers and resistants and Major de Guelys (*sic*) is listed with other members of the TILLEUL mission Indeed, Colonel RIVIER played the lead role in the ceremony and it is possibly he who is pinning the decoration on James Edgar.

Both Bob Maloubier and James Edgar – who were at the ceremony – were

James Edgar receiving a Croix de Guerre at Limoges

pretty sure that Jacques was not there, and he is certainly not visible on any of the photographic documentation, all of which was viewed by the author in Limoges in 2002 with the late lamented Jacques Valery, who had been a resistant in his youth (d. 2011).

So just to complicate matters, here is my translation of part of a report that appeared in *La Patrie de l'Allier* on 26 September and relates to a ceremony that had taken place 'yesterday afternoon', i.e. 25 September, appropriately, in Vichy:

> Silently, as was their habit during the months spent in the Maquis, the men from the Limousin region marched through the streets of our city, yesterday afternoon.
>
> No one had been told about it. But still, several thousand inhabitants gathered in the Place de l'Hôtel de Ville and in the main streets.
>
> Forming a horseshoe in front of the Mairie were a thousand men – nine companies of the Corrèze-Limousin group. The different organisations, in their

various uniforms, mingling. To the left, at the bottom of the steps, a police band. To the right the flag and its guardian. As it flapped in the wind, FLA, AS, Limoges could be discerned in its folds.

Among the personalities present were M. Jean Barbier, the Mayor, Commandant François, Major de Guélis of the British Army and Captain Simon of the AF [?RAF…]. The troops were commanded by Colonel Joly, and it was he who read the citations and pinned the Croix de Guerre on about 20 recipients.

Vichy, 25 Sept. 1945. March past Town Hall (PC)
Jacques extreme right with André Simon, the two nurses and Ian Mackenzie to his right

But by the afternoon of 25 September, Jacques and Simon (AF – the rank of Flight-Lieutenant is the RAF's equivalent rank of the Army's Captain) – were over in Vichy, and in a photo of the event, the former can be clearly discerned on the steps, taking the salute at the march-past, just as he had told his mother.

So how is it possible to explain these inconsistencies? The ones relating to the earlier ceremony are quite easy to explain: Jacques and Simon were still out in the field on 17 September, where fighting was still going on and lives being lost. So it may be that operational necessity compelled them to miss the first ceremony and arrangements were made for them to receive their decorations later. What has complicated matters is the above-mentioned report in *Visages de la Resistance*, places Jacques and Simon at the ceremony in Limoges. But Bisset died an accidental death involving a gun in Vichy on 24 September, so it may be that Jacques and Simon were also informed of his death, and felt duty-bound to get across to Vichy with all dispatch even though this meant missing any further ceremonies. The two men then decided to stay on in Vichy for the march-past of 25 September,[14] at which there were also awards made, including one to an Englishman – and then wait a few days longer in the hope of receiving instructions from London. When none came, they made their way to Paris and reported to EMFFI at Les Invalides and to SOE at the Hôtel Cecil.

The OSS Mission GERMINAL throws some light on this period:

(www.ibiblio.org/hyperwar/USMC/USMC-OSS/USMC-OSS-C)

Like Buckmaster's SOE Mission JUDEX (see below), the mission's object was to contact all US agents operating in SW France, so they were travelling round the region. Arriving in Limoges on 9 September 1944 they were receptioned by Major Staunton, Major de Guélis, Captain Fraser, Flt. Lt. Simon and 2nd Lt. Marcel. The OSS had taken over the former German Gestapo HQ in Limoges where the SOE agents were also staying. Jedburgh teams LEE and JAMES were also there.

On 24 September GERMINAL arrived in Vichy to learn of Bisset's accidental death. He had been preparing to leave for Paris in front of the Hotel des Ambassadeurs at about 13.00 hours when his Marlin sub-machine gun fell to the ground and went off and killed him. The following day the FFI formed a Guard of Honour outside the Hotel Radio with Allied officers acting as pall bearers. The body was taken to a small Protestant chapel where a brief ceremony was held.

He was buried at 10 am on 26 September and among the British and American officers present were Major Mackenzie and Major de Guélis.

The GERMINAL Mission then continued on its way southwards.

As it happened, Colonel Buckmaster was in Paris on his fact-finding mission (JUDEX HS7/134), and was able to greet Jacques and other returning agents before their return to London on 10 October. They also had an appointment with General Koenig, who received them most kindly. But probably Jacques' most joyful meeting in Paris was with his cousin, the ubiquitous Val Barbier, who had come up from the south. They toasted the occasion in champagne – they would never see one another again. Val returned to London on 27 Ocotober 1944.

For the planning of TILLEUL and the Mission's timetable see Appendix.

SUMMER INTERLUDE: A POSTSCRIPT

Late summer 1944. A gas- or charcoal-powered car known as a *gazogène* swept into the courtyard of a château a few miles south of Limoges. One of the daughters of the château watched as 'big' Uncle Jacques got out of the car, followed by his wireless operator, young James Edgar (who hadn't a clue where he was), and Teddy Bisset.

The 'big' uncle was, of course, Jacques Vaillant de Guélis, a cousin of the family and a member of SOE's Mission TILLEUL which had landed not that far away in the small hours of 8 July 1944. James watched as Jacques went to pray in the little chapel to the left of the entrance to the château and then followed him inside. The *chatelaine* was alone and embraced Jacques, and they went into the drawing-room to talk. The chatelaine was Solange de Neuville whose husband Louis Dufour de Neuville (born 1905) was to die on 16 November of that year, age thirty-nine. James sat a little apart with his Sten across his knee, while Bisset remained outside. Presently they were given something to eat, perhaps in the green-carpeted dining-room next door, where the walls were hung with green tapestries, so James remembered. Then the little girl took James outside into the garden while the cousins talked.

Fast forward sixty-two years. Jacques' wartime career is being researched and letters elicit various clues, one of which is the address of James Edgar, now in his nineties and living in Australia. He writes describing his visit to the mysterious château all those years ago. Where was it? Are you that little girl? Alas no, but perhaps we can find out who she was. Did they go to Bas Soleil, the home of Phillippe de Vomécourt? Definitely not, said the relative who now owns Jacques' manor house in Herry, not far from Sancerre. It must have been Solange de Neuville (née Gosset) at the Château de Combas, a few miles south of Limoges. She was a cousin of Jacques and helped the Resistance. The family were staunch Royalists and Catholics and had hidden Jews on their estate. Solange de Neuville died in 2005, aged 100.

On a warm September day in 2006, we, the author and her husband passed through the village of Vicq sur Breuilh and turned down the long drive to the Château de Combas, past the beautiful Limousin cattle bred by the then owner, Louis de Neuville, and into the same courtyard as James Edgar all those years ago. The ivy that he remembered has been taken down and perhaps the chapel is a bit shabbier, but in essence it remains the same. The Great Storm of 1999 felled many of the trees on the estate, but to the newcomer's eyes the château is surrounded by beautiful woods. Wolves once roamed here, as the heads in the hallway testify.

Solange de Neuville with her husband Louis, on leave *c.* 1944 (CdeN)

Waiting to greet us is Chantal Eva de Neuville, one of Solange's two daughters, who must have been the little girl of the story, then aged twelve, for she remembers a car sweeping into the courtyard. Her sister-in-law, Mme de Neuville, invites us into the drawing-room, where the rooms have not been much changed, though there is no sign of the green carpet that James remembers. But the views from the windows are brilliantly green and the tapestries on the dining-room walls are also green. James was right to remember this lovely place.

During the war they lived in fear – fear of betrayal, fear of the Germans turning up to search the place. But peace has descended once more and the worry now is how to afford a new roof.

And we thought: how extraordinary! We were reliving an old man's memories, answering his questions that were more than a half a century old and being welcomed by the relatives of 'big' Uncle Jacques who was 6ft 3in tall and my mother's first cousin.

As a result, James and Valerie Edgar flew to France from Australia and had an emotional reunion with that little girl, now in her seventies, at the Château de Combas.

Châteaux de Combas

Notes to Chapter 5

Louis Robert Eugène Monguilan alias Commandant Louis Thomas alias
MINIMUM

b. 1902

St Cyr, St Maisent, Polytechnique.

Regular Army – joined 27 May 1922, age 21

7th Regiment of Colonial Artillerie till BCRA Algiers in 22.2.1944 then by air to
BCRA London on 14.3.1944

2 Missions to France: TILLEUL and SHINOILE

He trained at the English schools including parachute drops.

Decorations: Chevalier de la Légion d'Honneur (1939) and 2 Croix de Guerre
one with 3 citations.

His pseudo with family details: BOYER

Then DGER after the war.

PF: HS9/1050

(Major-General) John K Singlaub OSS

US Army, 1st Lieut.

He had been trained in the US by Major William Ewart Fairburn in weapons and unarmed combat – Fairburn and Sykes had invented the 'Fairburn-Sykes' knife for hand to hand fighting. See *Hazardous Duty – An American Soldier in the 20th Century* with Malcolm McConnell (Simon and Schuster)

Team JAMES: Singlaub, Jacques Lebel de Penguilly (US Sergeant) and Anthony Denneau (sergeant, Radio)

Captain Claude Wauthier-Wurmser b. 28.9.1910

St Cyr. Mobilised 1939, escaped to French North Africa and returning to France via the Pyrenees, captured by the Spanish. Escaped again to England in 1941 and join the 3rd Regiment of SAS parachutists and then joined the staff of the 18th American Parachute Army Corps.

FOOTNOTES

[1] See also Wikipédia, Massacre de Tulle.

[2] Of the 156,000 Allied troops who landed in Normandy on D-Day, 4,414 were killed and there are no reliable figures for those wounded and missing. Although there are no official figures for D-Day on its own, Allied casualties throughout the Normandy campaign are estimated at 209,000.

[3] RAF Harrington, five miles west of Kettering, Northamptonshire, was built by American Engineers and opened as USAAF Station 179 on 25 March 1944. The first operational squadron to use the new station was the 801st Bombardment Group (Provisional), known as 'The Carpetbaggers' because of its crews' involvement in clandestine missions over Occupied Europe. The 801st were merged with 492nd Bombardment Group (Heavy) in August 1944.

[4] Teddy Bisset-HS9/158/2. James Edgar – HS9,468/9. – Circuit mission reports 1944 HS6/587 the National Archives.

[5] Ibid.

[6] A Gaullist by persuasion, General Koenig had won great respect as a military commander at the Battle of Bir Hakeim (26 May – 11 June 1942), when his First French Brigade (3,700 men) had held its ground for 16 days against 5 Axis divisions (*c.* 50,000 men). If anyone could unite the different factions of the FFI, it was Koenig.

[7] Known by several code names, including Rivière, Robert, Auriac and Marcel, Louis-Marcel Godefroy had a very distinguished career as a highly active member of the Resistance that went back to 1940. In his capacity as Head of the FTPP in the Corrèze, it was he who had organised the harassment of the Division *Das Reich* as it tried to move northwards between 8 and 12 June 1944.

[8] Mme Sauviat told the author this when she visited Chadebac. The 'message personnel' sent to the Sauviats was '*Marie-Louise n'aime pas les mandarines*'.

[9] Letter from James Edgar to the author 2002.

[10] Letter of 2002 from James Edgar to the author.

[11] HS9/1362/2.

[12] Letter of 2002 from James Edgar to the author.

[13] The SAS leader Captain Claude Wauthier and his men were receptioned by the *maquisards* and contacted de Guélis and Thomas.

[14] De Guélis did not mention the march-past in Vichy in his report, but he did tell his mother that he had 'taken the salute' there, and indeed there he was on the extreme right of a photo on the steps of the Town Hall. Also there were Janine Nussbaumer and Georgett Chapbrerie as well as André Simon. In an article in la *Patrie de l'Allier* on 26 September, 1944 a commandant JACQUES is among the recipients of awards in Vichy along with Colonel Joly and 18 others.

6

GERMANY AND AFTER
(JANUARY–AUGUST 1944)

*Capable and courageous. A man of strong
personality, not too easy to control.*

Major-General C. M. McVerson Gubbins,
January–December 1945
(Comments in Jacque's personal file) at the National Archives

Once back from Paris, Jacques, now considered a highly experienced officer, was, together with Major Nicholas R. Bodington and Major Watt, transferred on the orders of General Gubbins to SOE's X (Germany) Section on 28 December 1944. He was immediately attached to S[pecial] P[lanning] U[nit] 47 in Brussels, the forward SOE mission on European soil, which was attached to the Supreme Headquarters Allied Expeditionary Force and so under the overall command of General George ('Bobby') Erskine (1899–1965), the brilliant commander of the 7th Armoured Division in North Africa (1943–44). Although the unit's major task was the re-interviewing of agents who had exfiltrated from Germany during the run-up to the Allied break-out from the Low Countries that would take place in the New Year, it was also tasked with helping the Belgian Government to demobilise the Resistance movement that SOE had helped to create and with taking part in the technical interrogation of prisoners. For at least the first two months of this latest attachment, Jacques' immediate superior in the Brussels SOE was Lieutenant-Colonel (later Sir) Hardy Amies (1909–2003), the future official dress-designer for Queen Elizabeth II. Amies had joined SOE in spring 1941 as an Acting Captain in the Intelligence Corps and worked in T (Belgium and Luxembourg) Section until September 1944, when he assumed command of SPU 47.

But this posting may also have been due to the fact that Jacques and Bodington were personae non gratae in France.[1] Certainly, in view of what Dodds-Parker had hinted about them, it would have been in SOE's best interests if both officers were formally prohibited from going to France without prior permission.[2] Jacques had fallen foul of de Gaulle, at least from his time in Algiers with Massingham, and de Gaulle was unforgiving to say the least. And not only had there been doubts about Bodington's loyalty, he had an unfortunate manner which had upset people in France – where he wanted to apply for a post. So a letter in Bodington's SOE file of 10 March 1945 places both Jacques and Bodington in Brussels, working for D/INTER or AD/Z and responsible to a Commander Johns. It was in Belgium, too, that Jacques met Major Vernon Mallinson, and he, in a censored letter of 26 April 1945 on quite another matter, wrote to Jacques' uncle, Professor Paul Barbier, that 'Jack de Guélis was great fun whilst he was with us. He came out in January of this year, stayed about ten weeks and then was whisked back to London HQ. I have heard nothing more of his movements since'.[3] One of the returning agents that Jacques interviewed or debriefed in January 1945, was Belgian s/Lieutenant *au corps des Agents de Renseignement et d'Action*, Adolphe Shoemackers. Jacques must have made a powerful and lasting impression on the man because, many years later, in a letter of 10 June 1951, he wrote a very touching letter to Jacques' widow about him, and begged for a photo. (Family letter)

Alhough SFU 47 was not closed down until 6 June 1945, Jacques returned to England and the SOE pool on 22 March 1945. Here, he was promptly reassigned to the Special Allied Air Reconnaissance Force (SAARF), which existed between 25 March and 1 July 1945 and about which very little is known, probably because it was formed in a great hurry and achieved relatively little. But Sir James Hutchinson (1893–1979) – 'the Pimpernel of the Maquis' – who had had plastic surgery because his face was known to the Gestapo, had been a member of a Jedburgh team and worked for SOE's RF Section, has something to say about it at the end of his book *That Drug Danger* (1977, pp. 176–180). The unit was made up mainly of SOE and OSS personnel, together with members of other special forces, largely British, American and French, and training was provided by SOE and OSS officers at their HQ at Wentworth Golf Course, near Virginia Water. Brigadier J. S. Nicholls was in command, with Colonel John Tyson of OSS representing the

American members. There was a British NAAFI and an American PX, and the trainees had the use of the golf course, swimming pool and tennis courts.[4] Many SOE agents from an impressive range of nationalities who, like Jacques, had already emerged from their clandestine activities in Europe and made their way back to Britain, found themselves recruited by SAARF. Hutchinson, for instance, names Major Patrick ('Paddy') Leigh-Fermor (1915–2011), who is best-known for his activities on Crete, especially the abduction of General Heinrich Kreipe (1895–1976) between 26 April and 14 May 1944, and Colonel Francis Cammaerts (see note 3, Ch. 3), another man who was 6ft 4in tall and fresh from his successes, not to mention his providential escape from the Germans, in the South of France (*A Pacifist at War* by Ray Jenkins, 2009, pp. 198–200).[5]

The three-man teams were to be made up of 32 British, including 12 from MO1 (SP), 32 US including 6 from OSS, 40 French, 10 Belgian and 6 Polish. One team was to go to Czechoslovakia for special work there. No other mention is made of this.

The final phase of the war in the west, the Allies' rapid advance into Germany after their break-out eastwards from Holland and through the *Reichswald*, began on 22 February 1945. SAARF was organised in its wake and with some haste because the Allied chiefs were becoming increasingly worried that, as the war drew to a close, the inmates of POW and concentration camps might be executed or moved about and decided to put a rescue mission in place. As we shall shortly see, this fear was, to some extent, justified, especially as regards the concentration camps in the East, where such measures had already begun. Germany was certainly not a safe place at the time since clandestine guerrillas and genuine vigilantes were already at large. But beginning in late February/early March 1945, an even greater threat was posed, in the view of the Allied Commanders, that the Nazis' plans for *Unternehmen Werwolf* (Operation Werewolf) was a reality.[6] Established in October 1944 with *SS-Obergruppenführer* Hans-Adolf Prützmann (1901–45), an expert in partisan tactics, as its guiding light, the aim of the operation was to recruit thousands of fanatical young Nazis as Werewolves, train and equip them for guerrilla warfare, and, ultimately, concentrate them in an 'Alpine Redoubt' in Bavaria where they would carry out a last, suicidal stand (Beevor, 2002, pp. 173–4). The idea was fostered by Dr Goebbels from about mid-March 1945, and his public support reached its height in the *Werwolf-Rede* (Werewolf-Speech) that he broadcast from his *Werwolfsender* (Station Werewolf) of 23 March 1945. Here, he appealed to the werewolves of Berlin and Brandenburg to rise against the enemy and fight to the death on behalf of 'the National Socialist revolution' now that the 'cowards and traitors' had left Berlin and the *Führer* had decided to remain there (Beevor, 2002, pp. 261–2). A week later, on the not inappropriate day of 1 April 1945, an appeal was broadcast to the entire German people to become a member and fight the Allies under the motto of 'Conquer or die' (Beevor, 2002, pp. 173–4). *Unternehmen Werwolf* may have gradually proved over the next months to be a myth.

After VE-Day, another (growing) hazard was the large numbers of displaced persons and former inmates of labour camps who left their camps and began to roam the countryside. And there was also the enduring danger of booby-traps, one of which killed Jacques' cousin Major Raoul Paul Cuthbert Hepburn near Cologne on 17 November 1945: a wire stretched across the road along which his jeep was travelling may well have decapitated him, since that is what such devices were designed to do. As Professor M. R. D. Foot put it: at the 'tag end of the War', Germany 'was still full of roughs who had not yet learned peaceable ways'.[7] So the original idea behind SAARF was to drop three-man teams *à la* Jedburgh into Germany near to the prison camps in order to negotiate with their commandants and secure the safety of the inmates. Accordingly, Hutchinson tells us, SAARF agents went into Germany carrying anti-typhus serum for those inmates (1977, p.177) But the teams also took with them an index of missing SOE agents and were charged to find out what had become of them.

Quite by chance, two lists of SAARF three-man teams have been preserved by the Imperial War Museum. Their leaders include Captain Auguste Floiras, Major G. Goldsmith, Major Howard Gunn of F Section, Krystyna Skarbek's (see note 9) friend Captain A. Koworski-Kennedy and Paul Aussaresses, not forgetting Mme Julien, the wireless operator for the PERMIT circuit. But the list also includes Jacques, who is not mentioned anywhere else in connection with the unit. Indeed, when one SAARF survivor was asked, he was sure that Jacques was not one of them. Moreover, his SOE file is very vague about the last months of his life and it certainly makes no mention of SAARF. Nevertheless, a search at the National

Archives produced two files that were somewhat more informative and proved unquestionably that Jacques' involvement with the mysterious unit was true.[8] The suspicion that Jacques' personal file at the National Archives has been well and truly 'weeded' leads one to wonder what his team was really up to. Going back to his escape from France in 1940/41, no report is to be found either, and any information about his rescue from Spain has gone.

Philip Worrall (SW)

Only one SAARF airborne mission actually took place – OPERATION VIOLET, led by the extraordinary Major Philip Worrall (1913–2005) when six teams were dropped near Stalag XIA (Altengrabow POW Camp), near the village of Dörnitz outside Magdeburg, en route to Berlin, on 26 April 1945. On that date and again on 3 May, Jacques and his team (code-name FOLDER), consisting of Lieutenant F. G. Maynard and Sergeant A. A. Nicholl (wireless operator), were standing by at Wentworth. Parachutes were abandoned and jeeps were to be used on future missions. But, on 7 May, i.e. one day before VE-Day, Jacques' team and one led by Major Dennis ('Jumbo') Newman left RAF Harrington (USAAF Station 179; see note 3, Ch. 5) with orders to proceed to SPU47 in Brussels, and there collect 15cwt trucks, a movement order that would allow them to travel in the vast area now held by General Omar Bradley's 12th Army Group,[9] and instructions to proceed to selected camps. At the same time, intensive searches were being made for such fanatical and prominent Nazis as Major Weinberger, the Flak Liaison Officer for the Magdeburg area, who was supposed to be under secret orders concerning *Werwolf* preparations.

Newman and Jacques decided to split up and each take a particular area.[10] Jacques and his team decided to go about 180 miles south-eastwards, in the direction of the mythical Alpine Redoubt and, more significantly, KZ-Flossenbürg in Bavaria, about seven miles west of the Czech border, one of the less remembered of Germany's larger concentration camps that was almost certainly one of the 'selected camps' on the team's orders. Set up by the SS in 1938, it had numbered *c.* 96,000+ inmates at its height, of whom *c.* 30,000 died from arbitrary shootings, disease, under-nourishment and forced labour in factories and quarries. Whether FOLDER knew it or not, it was going to a place that was just as appalling as the more notorious Buchenwald or Dachau.

On 6 September 1944, the French-Canadian SOE agent Gustave Daniel Alfred Biéler (1904–44) (code-name GUY), the organiser of the Musician network in France, was executed there by firing-squad after being arrested by the Gestapo on 13 January 1944 and subjected to consistent and brutal interrogation under torture in various prisons. On 29 March 1945, thirteen more SOE agents were hanged there. On 9 April 1945, several prominent members of the German Resistance met the same fate there – including the Theologian Dr Dietrich Bonhoeffer (1906–5), Admiral Wilhelm Canaris (1887–1945), the Head of German Military Intelligence, and his Deputy General Hans Oster (1887–1945). On 20 April 1945, the camp administration decided to march 22,000 of the 'fit' inmates towards KZ-Dachau, a good 140 miles to the south-south-west, during which 7,000 of those who had set out died or were brutally killed. So when the US 90th ('Tough Ombres') and 97th ('Trident') Divisions liberated KZ-Flossenbürg on 23 April 1945, it contained just 1,600 sick and dying inmates, mainly in the hospital blocks.[11] Perhaps, therefore, Jacques' team had been sent to the area to investigate the camp records or even look for suspected Nazi criminals who were connected with the camp. But when, at about 16.30 hours on 16 May, they were on duty and travelling westwards in a captured German vehicle along the road from Flossenbürg to the picturesque market town of Weiden in der Oberpfalz, about 20 miles away, a small camouflaged car suddenly pulled out of a concealed side-road about 20 yards ahead. In their reports, Lieutenant Maynard and Sergeant Nicholl identified its driver as a German civilian called Dietrich who was working in the camp. Maynard, who was driving at about 35mph, braked and swerved to avoid the German vehicle. But 'Dietrich' took his hands off the wheel, started screaming and accelerated in an apparent attempt to cut across the British car, whereupon his car hit the near-side door of the British vehicle, causing it to somersault and overturn. All three men were thrown out onto the roadway, but Jacques, who must have been sitting on the near-side next to Maynard the driver, was probably already seriously injured by the impact. Maynard, who was shaken but not hurt, sent Nicholl, who had sustained a fracture of the left hand and a dislocated thumb, to summon an ambulance which rushed Jacques to the 39th Evacuation Hospital at Weiden). Their accident reports, it is interesting to note, although very brief, were not written until 27 May 1945.[12]

In Marie de Guélis' letter to her brother Paul of 19 June 1945, she wrote that two American surgeons had devotedly cared for him throughout the night without morphine or other pain relief. His injuries, she said included ten broken ribs, some vertebra and his right thigh. Back in hospital in Lichfield, he told his mother he would never forget what the Americans had done for him. The belief in the family that the collision was no accident is understandable, given the fact the other vehicle was driven by a worker from Flossenberg and that Jacques' team were very probably returning from the camp because in his report Sgt. Nicolls, who sustained a fractured thumb, says he was first treated at Flossenburg Camp hospital and later at the 39th US Evacuation Hospital. The thought that occurs is that they had actually been or were across the border in Czechoslovakia because his mother thought that was where the accident happened and she also wrote that he had been flown to Paris where his wife could visit him every day (letter from Marie de Guélis to her brother).

Reichsbund der Deutschen Beamten (RDB.) e. V.

Kreis Weiden-Neustadt a. W.-N.   Weiden (Obpf.)

Abteilung:

Zeichen, Nr.:

Anlagen:

Ihr Schreiben vom: Ihr Zeichen: Mein Schreiben vom: Weiden (Opf.)

Betrifft:

SUBJECT: STATEMENT OF ACCIDENT.

By. 2755518 Sgt Nicoll. A.

SIR, -

On 16th of May 1945 at approximately 1630 hrs we were proceeding from FLOSSENBERG to WEIDEN by car. The approx speed of our vehicle was about 35 MPH. As we were descending a small gradient I saw a car appear out of a small concealed side road about 20 yds in front of our vehicle. Lt. Maynard who was driving our car immediately braked and swerved to avoid the other car. The driver of the other car who was a German civilian accelerated and tried to cut across in front of us. The civilian then took his hands off the steering wheel & started screaming.

The car struck our car on the near side door and our car somersaulted on to its side and we were thrown out on to the roadway clear of the car. I found Major De Guellis lying beside a fence post and I turned him on to his back and saw he was badly injured, just then Lt Maynard told me to fetch a doctor and an ambulance which I did. I sustained a fracture of the left hand and dislocated thumb for which I was treated at Flossenburg Camp Hospital and later at 39 U.S. EVAC HOSP.

SIGNED. A Nicoll Sgt 27 May 45

Accident Report (TNA)

Above: Philip Worrall in peaked hat with Sgt. Nicoll in an army truck after Worrall had taken over from Jacques (SW)

Below: Group – Worrall seated second right, Maynard standing left and Nicoll in beret (SW)

By the time of the accident, Major Worrall had completed OPERATION VIOLET and was back in Brussels. He was then ordered to Weiden to collect Jacques' papers and take over from him. Major Newman, the leader of the second team, told Worrall that both teams were free to enter concentration camps and labour camps at will but stressed that their real job was to set up a base and wait for London to radio information about agents and operators who were still unaccounted for. Neither team had had much success and both were rather disillusioned – which is very strange, given the list of SOE casualties in Flossenbürg.

According to Major Newman's report to Col. Ingham Clarke (see note 12) on Monday 14 July, after deciding to split up and cover different areas, they reported to G2 First Army in Weimar still using our 'T' Force story.

Major Worrall's account (from part of his memoir *Surviving Without a Father* given to the author) is that his movement order was:

> ... you will proceed on Thursday 24th May 1945 to the 39 US Evacuation Hospital, Weiden and contact Major J de Guélis and take over from him any papers relevant to his Missions. You will then contact the remaining members of his Mission with T/Force and take over command. On completion of your mission, you will report back to SPU Belgium.

So, Major Worrall understandably assumed that these two teams were part of T Force which was an entirely different operation: an elite British Army Force also operating in the final stages of World War II, tasked with securing military and scientific intelligence and later seeking out Nazi scientists and other top men before the US or Russian authorities could lay their hands on them ... or, the thought occurs that the mission was not what it seemed.

Newman visited Jacques in hospital in Weiden towards the end of May, when he seemed to be recovering. The report (see appendix) from the 39th Evacuation Hospital was dated 27 May 1945 and states that 'evacuation will take place on the 28th thru (*sic*) regular channels. It seems likely that he was then flown to Paris, as his mother believed, before being flown home to the Emergency Hospital, Burntwood Road, Lichfield, where, however, he contracted an infection and died on 7 August 1945.

His funeral took place at St John's Church, Cardiff, and he is buried in Cathays Cemetery, Cardiff, near the graves of his mother and grandparents. His headstone was the regulation War Graves design and the Imperial War Graves Commission

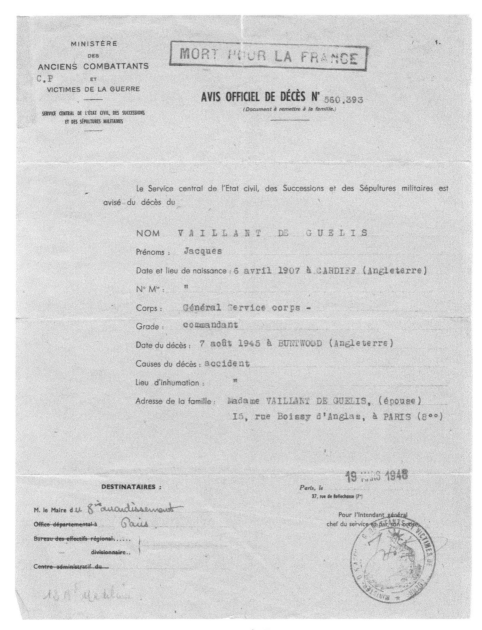

Mort pour la France

Jacques' grave in Cathays Cemetery Cardiff

undertook to look after it in perpetuity. Now, the Commonwealth War Graves Commission have taken on the responsibility and inspect headstones from time to time. If needed, they are repaired or replaced.

As so often in Jacques' war-time history, there is something curious about the circumstances of his death. Lieutenant Maynard names the driver of the other car as Dietrich, but then we hear no more about him, whether he was injured, killed or arrested. Almost two years later, on 6 March 1947, the Commander of the British War Crimes Group sent a list of eight ex-Flossenbürg camp guards to the US War Crimes Liaison Group, asking in which they were interested and which could be released. Among them is a Wilhelm Dietrich, who had worked at KZ-Leitmeritz just across the border in Czechoslovakia, one of Flossenbürg's many satellite camps, KZ-Theresienstadt, the so-called 'model Ghetto' in

Czechoslovakia that was used as the set for propaganda photographs and one (uncompleted) propaganda film, showing the idealised conditions in which Jewish deportees allegedly lived after their transportation to the East, and, of course, KZ-Flossenbürg itself. So was this Dietrich the same man as the civilian driver?[13] And did he have something to hide, such as complicity in the brutal events that were part of KZ-Flossenbürg's everyday routine, or the execution of the German *Prominenten* and the SOE agents? Certainly, no-one called Dietrich was on the list of officers and guards at Flossenbürg who were tried by US Military Court at Dachau between 12 June 1946 and 19 January 1947.

Did a SAARF team actually go into Czechoslovakia? Was this Jacques, the man who was 'not easy to control', deciding to visit one of KZ-Flossenbürg's satellite camps? The FOLDER team may not have been undertaking such a foray on the day of Jacques' death since the team's car was travelling westwards, away from Czechoslovakia but they can't have been far from Flossenburg if Sgt Nicolls was initially treated at the camp hospital. But would it have been significant if they had been doing so, since the border with Czechslovakia had ceased to exist in October 1938 when the Germans incorporated the largely German-speaking Sudetenland that lined its western frontier into the Third Reich. Moreover, on 16 May 1945, the whole of the Sudetenland and the western end of largely Czech-speaking Bohemia were still occupied by Patton's 3rd Army, making 3,485 square miles of territory technically part of the territory controlled by the 12th Army Group within which Mission FOLDER had a permit to travel.[14] And even though Reynolds, Jacques' driver from the period of phoney war (Chapter 2), said in a posthumous eulogy that consists of an undated typescript in the family papers, that the collision was not an accident,[15] silence surrounds the event. When asked by the author, neither Worrall nor Newman appear to have heard such a suggestion, or if they knew more, they said nothing. But all the members of his family believed that Jacques's death was not an accident – though perhaps this was solely because of Reynold's eulogy. But it does seem strange that the accident was never discussed, even with the drivers.[16]

But then, Jacques' story is full of so many false claims and contradictions. Perhaps he was parachuted into Corsica – or perhaps he was not. He went into Cannes by submarine to help rebuild destroyed SOE networks – or was it Bodington who went instead? He was awarded a medal at a ceremony in Limoges – but was in Vichy on that date. After Mission TILLEUL he was reported as having proceeded towards the Rhine with the French Army – but he couldn't have done as he went back to London from Paris. Someone is sure that they saw him with another SOE agent who was known to them among a group of 'ruffians' in a pub in Saffron Walden in 1940 or 1941, and they whispered that they were off on a mission![17] In the *Grand Prix Saboteurs* (p. 107) a similar story of a mission to kidnap German Officers surfaces and there are others though the authorities always denied such raids took place. Where and how did Reynolds acquire his information on the accident which, possibly, was no accident? Enquiries have turned up nothing. It is a fact that Jacques' cousin Raoul Duncan, father of a baby girl, was killed in Germany by a wire stretched across the road, that threw him out of the vehicle. (A letter to his widow from his commanding officer.) So, MRD Foot was right in that there were unruly elements at large in Germany at the time. (Letter to the author, 28 March 2005.) How are we to reconcile the official report that Jacques was treated in an evacuation hospital in Weiden when his mother believed that he was flown to Czechoslovakia for treatment and that his wife was with him? Unless he was moved from Weiden when he had improved and his mother was unaware of it as seems most likely.

But then, so much was destroyed. One enquiry to the son of an SOE agent elicited the response that his father, like other former agents, had destroyed all his papers. Not long before his death in 2003, Sir Hardy Amies declined to give out any information on his work with the SOE. Nor were agents supposed to keep personal documents, though some, like 'Xan' Fielding in Crete, did just that.[18] Just after the end of the war, some documents and orders must have seemed highly controversial, dangerous even, and were binned. But as Vera Atkins said at the time: nobody dreamed that anyone would be interested after the war. Moreover, when writing his first edition of *S.O.E. in France*, part of the Government's Official History of World War II, Professor Michael Foot was not permitted to keep notes of his unpublished references, and even in the updated edition of 2004, when so much has come into the public domain, there are still gaps in his sources.[19]

And yet there are surprising survivals: Major Andrew Croft (1906–1998) kept everything: photos and orders, which include his orders to meet Major Gilles on Corsica – just another tiny piece of the jigsaw that is now Jacques' life.[20]

Jacques in uniform with cigar

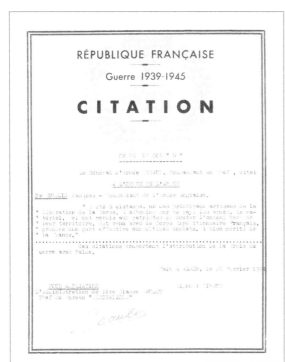

Citation for Croix de Guerre

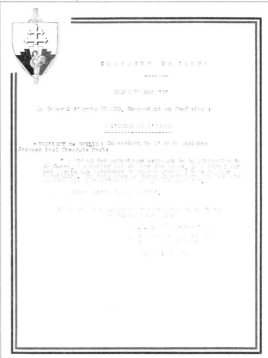

FOOTNOTES

---

[1] Bodington's Personal file (HS9/171/1).

[2] Bodington's Personal file (HS9/171/1).

[3] Letter from Major Vernon Mallinson, of 26 April 1945 to Prof. Paul Barbier (Family letters).

[4] HS7/20.

[5] On 13 August 1944, Cammaerts, Alexander Wallace ('Xan') Fielding (1918–91), one of Leigh-Fermor's collaboratos on Crete, and a French agent called Christian Sorensen were arrested in Digne, Southern France, by the Gestapo who possibly did not know the importance of their haul. A young, but extremely successful Polish operative named Krystyna Skarbek (1905–52) – known also as Christine Granville – got them released by arguing with two Gestapo officers for three hours: an Alsation called Albert Schenck and a Belgian called Max Waen. She told them all kind of stories – that she was married to Cammaerts and a niece of General Montgomery, and that when the invasion came she would see that they were handed over to an avenging French population if they did not get the three British agents released. The terrified collaborators complied.

[6] Judging by what Beevor has to say, the Russians were even more convinced of the veracity of this myth – or if not its veracity, then its usefulness (2002, pp. 175, 260, 414 and 415).

[7] Letter from Professor M. R. D. Foot to the author 28 March 2005.

[8] Reports of the accident and a hospital report in the rather meagre files of SAARF in the National Archives. Duxford archives were hardly more informative on of this short-lived organisation HS7/20 and HS7/21.

[9] Consisting of the US 1st, 3rd, 9th and 15th Armies and 1.3 million men by the end of the war, the US 12th Army Group controlled France, Belgium, Holland and much of Germany by this time.

[10] HS7/20.

[11] KZ-Dachau, to the north of Munich, was liberated by the US 42nd ('Rainbow') and 45th ('Thunderbird') Divisions on 29 April 1945. By then, it still contained 32,000 prisoners. At the time of the liberation of KZ-Flossenbürg, both US Divisions were in XII Corps, commanded by Lieutenant-General Stafford LeRoy Irwin (1893–1955). On 30 April, i.e. a day *after* the liberation, 97th Division was moved into V Corps, commanded by Lieutenant General Clarence R. Huebner (1888–1972).

[12] Reports dated 27 May 1945 by Maynard and Nicholls (HS7/20 and 21) and a meeting with the late Philip Worrall of 2005.

[13] WO309/2054.Flossenburg Concentration Camp, Germany-Detention of guards and release of alleged war criminals.

[14] On 4 May, Eisenhower gave Patton permission to invade former Czechoslovakia up to a line going north-south from Karlovy Vary to Plzeň, and then curving round eastwards to České Budejovice. The invasion began on 5 May, the liberation of the country took place on 6 May and the line had been reached, and in some cases crossed, by 7 May. The Soviet Army moved in from the East on 9 May. Irwin's XII Corps did not pull out of Czechoslovakia until the end of May, and Huebner's V Corps had not completely left until mid-June.

[15] Reynold's eulogy, undated and purpose unknown. Among then family papers.

[16] Letter of 2005 from Philip Worrall.

[17] Story told to the author by Jon Wilson about this incident in 1941 or 42.

[18] These later became his *Hide and Seek: The Story of a War-time Agent* (London: Secker and Warburg, 1955) – a collector's item.

[19] A French translation of *S.O.E. in France* only appeared in 2008. The suggestion is that when it first appeared, the authorities did not want to upset de Gaulle, and even less so in 1966 when he was in power and Britain's entry into the Common Market was at stake. But in that way, he was able to create his own history of the Resistance. Now, the French will be able to read another side of their story and they will wonder why some SOE agents were never made agents of the Liberation and why de Guélis was not awarded the *Légion d'Honneur* proposed by General Henry Martin after the liberation of Corsica.(Only a typescript by an unknown admirer which may have been General Henri Martin survives among the family papers) Jacques would have been the fourth member of his family to earn this decoration. But did he die before it could be awarded or was it blocked by the General?

[20] Andrew Croft's papers. [Andrew Croft's daughter, Julia Korner donated some of his papers which were relevant to Corsica, to the A Bandera Museum in Ajaccio in 200 ?.

APPENDIX

GENEALOGY:
The de Guélis family tree

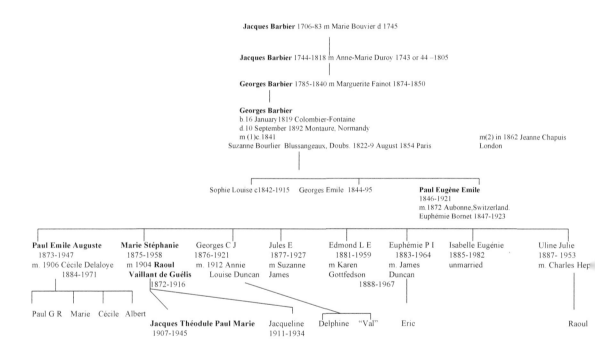

Jacques Barbier 1706-83 m Marie Bouvier d 1745

Jacques Barbier 1744-1818 m Anne-Marie Duroy 1743 or 44 –1805

Georges Barbier 1785-1840 m Marguerite Fainot 1874-1850

Georges Barbier
b.16 January1819 Colombier-Fontaine
d.10 September 1892 Montaure, Normandy
m (1)c.1841
Suzanne Bourlier Blussangeaux, Doubs. 1822-9 August 1854 Paris

m(2) in 1862 Jeanne Chapuis
London

Sophie Louise c1842-1915   Georges Emile 1844-95   **Paul Eugène Emile**
1846-1921
m.1872 Aubonne,Switzerland.
Euphémie Bornet 1847-1923

Paul Emile Auguste
1873-1947
m. 1906 Cécile Delaloye
1884-1971

Marie Stéphanie
1875-1958
m 1904 **Raoul
Vaillant de Guélis**
1872-1916

Georges C J
1876-1921
m. 1912 Annie
Louise Duncan

Jules E
1877-1927
m Suzanne
James

Edmond L E
1881-1959
m Karen
Gottfedson

Euphémie P I
1883-1964
m. James
Duncan
1888-1967

Isabelle Eugénie
1885-1982
unmarried

Uline Julie
1887- 1953
m. Charles Hep

Paul G R   Marie   Cécile   Albert

Jacques Théodule Paul Marie
1907-1945

Jacqueline
1911-1934

Delphine   "Val"   Eric

Raoul

162

The Barbier family tree

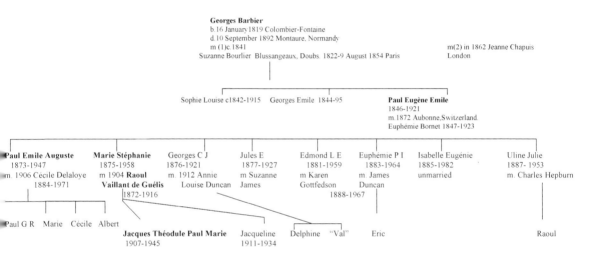

Georges Barbier
b.16 January 1819 Colombier-Fontaine
d.10 September 1892 Montaure, Normandy
m (1)c.1841
Suzanne Bourlier Blussangeaux, Doubs. 1822-9 August 1854 Paris

m(2) in 1862 Jeanne Chapuis
London

Sophie Louise c1842-1915 Georges Emile 1844-95 **Paul Eugène Emile**
1846-1921
m.1872 Aubonne,Switzerland.
Euphémie Bornet 1847-1923

Paul Emile Auguste 1873-1947 m. 1906 Cécile Delaloye 1884-1971	**Marie Stéphanie** 1875-1958 m 1904 **Raoul Vaillant de Guélis** 1872-1916	Georges C J 1876-1921 m. 1912 Annie Louise Duncan	Jules E 1877-1927 m Suzanne James	Edmond L E 1881-1959 m Karen Gottfedson	Euphémie P I 1883-1964 m. James Duncan 1888-1967	Isabelle Eugénie 1885-1982 unmarried	Uline Julie 1887- 1953 m. Charles Hepburn

Paul G R   Marie   Cécile   Albert

Jacques Théodule Paul Marie
1907-1945

Jacqueline
1911-1934

Delphine   "Val"   Eric

Raoul

When Paul Colonna d'Istria heard of Jacques's death and received a copy of his profile, he wrote to Val Barbier:

[…] et m n émotion fut grande q[uan]d j'aperçus son fidèle portrait – oui – Il est bien ainsi que n[ou]s le voyons q[uel]q[ue]fois, grave et doux, le regard lointain, comme à la poursuite d'un rêve, d'un idéal, dont il voulait faire une réalité.

C'est dans cet état d'âme, plein de générosité, de don de soi, de volonté réfléchi aussi que la mort l'a ravi à nos yeux, mais il demeure d[an]s nos pensées, comme je l'éspère ce lieu sacré que 'dans sa personne et dans son oeuvre' Jacques a tissé et fortifié jour après jour tout au long de sa vie. Puissent tous ses efforts et ceux conjugués de toute une multitude dont nous sommes, ne pas avoir été vains.

And when General Martin heard the same news he wrote to Jacques's widow:

[…] Le Major de Guélis m'accompagnait sur le contre-torpilleur Fantasque qui nous a transporté d'Alger à Ajaccio; il m'a souvent accompagné et aussi souvent précédé dans les montagnes de Corse au moment où nous refoulions les Allemands de la côte orientale de l'Ile. Dès que la Corse a été nettoyée, il nous a quittés pour préparer le débarquement en France, mais nous n'avons jamais oublié sa haute taille, son calme, sa finesse, sa sympathique compréhension de nos sentiments et les facilités que nous a donné, dans les premiers jours, le remarquable réseau de transmission organisé par lui entre la Corse et le Grand Quartier Allié d'Alger.

Sa réserve et la discrétion de son action si efficace ont fait qu'il n'a peut-être pas été récompensé comme je l'eusse souhaité. Je l'avais proposé pour une citation et la Légion d'Honneur. […] Le souvenir qu'il laisse à tous ceux qui l'ont vu à l'oeuvre reste celui d'une nature généreuse, d'un homme remarquablement complet et d'un camarade de combat singulièrement courageux.[1]

---

[1] Letter in the author's possession as is a scrap of paper with Colonna d'Istria's eulogy.

GLOSSARY

ANVIL	Allied invasion from the South of France
AS	Armée Secrète. Secret Army set up by de Gaulle
BCRA	Bureau central de Renseignement et d'Action.
CFLN (FCNL)	Comité Francais de Liberation National
CinC	Commander in Chief
CO	Commanding Officer
CLISSOLD	Acc to Hodgart he was part of this mission from September to October 1943.
CORSICAN	Mission to France 10 October 1941. Jean le Harivel was its radio operator.
Deuxième Bureau	French military intelligence agency
DMR	Délégué Militaire Régional. Gaullist chiefs of the Resistance in each region, eg.R5
DGER	Direction Générale des Etudes et Récherches
EMFFI	Etat-Major des Forces Françaises de l'Intérieur
ETA	Estimated time of arrival
F (SOE)	Special Operatons Executive. F section was independent and run by the British, RF section run by the French.
FFI	Forces Françaises de l'Intérieur. French forces in the Secret Army.
FTP	Francs-Tireurs et Partisans. Communist French Resistance
FOLDER	SAARF mission to Germany
GOC	General Officer Commanding
GSO2	General Staff Officer grade 2
MBE	Member of the Order of the Britsh Empire
MI5	Military Intelligence section 5, the UK's security service
MI6	The Secret Intelligence Service (SIS) commonly known as MI6. The UK government's foreign intelligence service.
ORA	Organisation de Résistance de l'Armée. Vichy replacement of the Armistice Army
OSS	The American Office of Strategic Services

OVERLORD	Allied invasion of Normandy
SAARF	Special Allied Airborne Reconnaissance Force. Short-lived force set up to investigate concentration camps
SHAEF	Supreme Headquarters Allied Expeditionary Force. Run by General Eisenhower
SHD	Service Historique de la Défense -Vincennes
STO	Service de Travail Obligatoire. Forced labour for the Germans which many men avoided by joining the resistance
STS	Special training Schools. Secret sites round the country used for SOE training
TORCH	Allied invasion of North Africa.
TRAPPER	The name given to TILLEUL in the planning stages
VESUVIUS	The liberation of Corsica

ACKNOWLEDGEMENTS

Firstly, I would like to thank David Harrison and Jon Wilson, who contacted me after I had written to the Special Forces Club. They gave me a great deal of useful information, as did Duncan Stuart, the SOE Adviser to the Foreign and Commonwealth Office. It turned out that Duncan Stuart's mother had been an Oxford friend of Jacques who was best man at her wedding. They have all continued to support me throughout, particularly David Harrison whose replies to queries were always so prompt. Roderick Bailey at the Imperial War Museum provided me with a list of people to contact and two lists of SAARF teams. I am also grateful to all the authors who were kind enough to reply to my queries, including Sir Martin Gilbert, Professor Michael Foot, Mark Seaman and Simon Sebag-Montefiore.

I am most grateful to the President and Fellows of Magdalen College, Oxford, the Churchill Archive Centre, Cambridge, the Keeper of the Royal Archives, Windsor, the Archivo Militar de Guadalafara, Spain, the British Embassy, Madrid, Jean-Pierre Girolami and the Musée A. Bandera, Ajaccio, Corsica and Dr Robin Darwall-Smith, Dr Roger Hutchins and Professor Richard Sheppard, all of Magdalen College, Oxford. Mervyn Joyner provided me with photos from Wrekin College, Shropshire, and my cousins Paul and Andrew Barbier kindly lent me family photographs and gave me information about the family.

My thanks are also due to Bruno Barthelot, John Coltman, Daniel Hymans, Alain de Vomécourt, Terry Hodgkinson, the late Bob Maloubier, Major Dennis Newman, Martyn Cox and the late Jacques Valéry. The late Philip Worrall welcomed me into his care home and gave me his account of visiting Jacques in hospital; Simon Worrall has helped me with photographs. James Edgar gave me insights into and photographs of Mission Tilleul. I talked briefly to the late Sir Douglas Dodds-Parker, Georges Connerade and Jean le Harivel, and Frances Cammaerts sent me a word. I am particularly grateful to the late Mme Sauviat, who chatted to me when I turned up unexpectedly in Chadebec, to David Gittins who drove me there and put me up, and to Major Andrew Croft's daughter Julia Korner, who allowed me to go through her father's papers. Thomas Ensminger of the 'Carpetbaggers' Association was particularly helpful in pinpointing wartime flights from RAF Harrington. Not forgetting Georgette Chabrerie and Dominique Seaux at St-Yrieix and Loic Lannou whose researches have produced some fascinating material and threw a little more light on Jacques' role. The late Bob Maloubier came down to Limoges from Paris specially to show us where Jacques had landed and other places in TILLEUL'S story. It was a privilege to spend time with him and listen to his reminiscences. There were so many others, on both sides of the Channel who helped me along the way with facts and photos; I would like to thank them all. Without them I could not have written this book.

Finally, my thanks to my publisher Ryan Gearing and editor/designer Vivian Head for their support. Special thanks also go to my son Daniel Isaaman.

DELPHINE ISAAMAN, 2017

Select Bibliography

Many of the books listed here include references to Jacques de Guélis.

For a more extensive Bibliography Google: *Liste bibliographique sur le SOE*

BOOKS

Alanbrooke, Field Marshal Lord, *War Diaries 1939–1945*, edited by Alex Danchev and Daniel Todman. London: Weidenfeld and Nicholson, 2001.

[Anon.], 'Guy Verstraete: Unsung Wartime Hero', in *Norwood Review*, no. 192 (Spring 2011), pp. 4–6.

Beevor, Antony, *The Fall of Berlin*. London: Penguin (Viking), 2002.

Binney, Marcus, *Secret War Heroes: Britain's Wartime Sabotage Organisation*. London: Hodder & Stoughton, 2005 [Includes short biographies of those involved].

Brockliss, Laurence W.B. (ed.), *Magdalen College, Oxford: A History* (Oxford: Magdalen College, 2008).

Brown, Anthony Cave, *Wild Bill Donovan: The Last Hero*. New York: Times Books, 1982.

Buckmaster, Maurice James, *Specially Employed: The Story of British Aid to French Patriots of the Resistance.* (London: Batchworth Press, 1952)

–––, *They Fought Alone: The Story of British Agents in France.* (London: Odhams, 1958).

Choury, Maurice, *Tous Bandits D'honneur: Résistance et Libéation de la Corse (juin 1940-octobre 1943)*. Paris: Éditions sociales, 1958.

Churchill, Peter, *Of their own Choice*. London: Hodder & Stoughton, 1952.

–––, *Duel of Wits.* London: Hodder & Stoughton, 1953.

–––, *The Spirit in the Cage.* London: Hodder & Stoughton, 1958.

Clark, Freddie, *Agents by Moonlight: The Secret History of RAF Tempsford during the Second World War.* Stroud: Tempus Publishing Ltd, 1999.

Cookridge, E. H., *Inside S.O.E.: The Story of Special Operations in Western Europe 1940–45.* London: Arthur Baker, 1966.

Corvo, Max, *OSS Italy 1942–45: A Personal Memoir of the Fight for Freedom.* New York: Enigma Books, 2005.

Couhat, Jean Labayle, *French Warships of World War II*. London: Ian Allan, 1971, pp. 52–60.

Craze, Michael M., *A History of Felsted School, 1564–1947.* Ipswich: Cowell, 1955.

Déricourt, Henri, *Espionage as a Fine Art,* trans. by Jean Overton Fuller from previously unpublished French original stories by Henri Déricourt, with an introduction and commentary. Norwich UK: Michael Russell, 1989.

de Vomécourt, Philippe, *Who Lived to See the Day.* London: Hutchinson, 1961.

Dodds-Parker, Douglas, *Setting Europe Ablaze: Some Accounts of Ungentlemanly Warfare.* London: Springwood, 1983.

Elliott, Geoffrey, *The Shooting Star.* London: Methuen, 2009.

Fleury, Georges and **Maloubier, Bob,** *Nageurs de Combat.* Paris: Éditions de la Table Ronde, 1989).

Fleutot, François-Martin, *Des Royalistes dans la Résistance.* Paris: Flammarion, 2000.

Foot, Michael Richard Daniell, *S.O.E. in France: An Account of the Work of the British Special Operations Executive in France* (Government Official Histories). London and Portland OR.: Whitehall History Publishing in Association with Frank Cass, 1966.

Frénay, Henri, *La Nuit finira: memoires de la Résistance, 1940-1945.* Paris: Michelon, 2006.

Fuller, Jean Overton, see **Déricourt, Henri.**

Funk, Arthur L., *Hidden Ally: The French Resistance, Special Operations, and the Landings in Southern France, 1944.* New York: Greenwood Press, 1952 [Now available on-line; an updated edition was published in 2004].

– – – , *The Politics of Torch: The Allied Landings and the Algiers Putsch.* Lawrence KS: Kansas UP, 1974,

Gambiez, Fernand, *Libération de la Corse.* Paris: Hachette, 1973.

Gaujac, Paul, *Special Forces in the Invasion of France.* Paris: Histoire et Collections, 2001.

Giraud, Henri, *Un seul but, la victoire: Algers 1942–44.* Paris: R. Juillard, 1949.

Jean Claude Guiet *Dead on Time.* The History Press, 2016.

Hoare, Samuel, *Ambassador on a Special Mission.* London: Collins, 1946.

Hodgkinson, Terry, 'Frederick' *La Mission Oubliée.* Larson Grove Press, 2007.

Hutchins, Roger and Sheppard, Richard, '[Jacques de Guélis]', in: *The Undone Years: Magdalen College Roll of Honour 1939–47 and Roll of Service 1939–1945.* Oxford: Magdalen College, pp. 82-9, 2004.

Hutchinson, James, *That Drug Danger.* Montrose (Scotland): Standard Press, 1977.

Janes, Peter Scott, *Conscript Heroes.* Boston, Lincs: Paul Mould Publishing, 2004.

Jenkins, Ray, *A Pacifist at War: The Life of Francis Cammaerts.* London: Hutchinson, 2009.

Jouanneau, Michel, *L'Organisation de la Résistance dans l'Indre. Juin 1940–1944.* (Limited edition printed in 1975 by l'Imprimerie Aubert, Versailles.

Langelaan, George, *Knights of the Floating Silk.* London: Hutchinson, 1959.

Lartégny, Jean, and **Maloubier, Bob,** *Triple jeu: l'espion Déricourt.* Paris: Éditions Robert Laffont, 1992.

Le Moigne, Louis, and **Barbanceys, Marcel,** *Sédentaires, réfractaires et maquisards: L'armée secrète en Haute Corrèze 1942-44.* Moulins: Éditions Association Amicale des Maquis A.S. Haute-Corrèze, 1979.

L'Herminier, Jean, *Casabianca.* Paris: Éditions France-Empire, 1953.

Long, Helen, *Safe Houses are Dangerous.* London: William Kimber & Co., 1985.

Loosely, Rhiannon, 'Paradise after Hell: the French Soldiers Evacuated from Dunkirk in 1940', *History Today*, 56(6) (June 2006), pp. 32-8.

Macintyre, Ben, *Operation Mincemeat.* London, Berlin, New York and Sydney: Bloomsbury, 2010.

Mackenzie, William J.M., *The Secret History of SOE: Special Operations Executive 1940–1945.* London: St Ermin's Press, 2002.

McCall, Gibb, *Flight Most Secret.* London: William Kimber & Co. Ltd, 1981.

Maloubier, Bob and **Fitère, Marie-Jean,** *Plonge dans l'or noir, espion.* Paris: Éditions Robert Laffont, 1986.

Marks, Leo, *Between Silk and Cyanide: A Codemaker's War.* London: Harper Collins, 1999.

Martin, Thomas, 'The Massingham Mission: SOE in French North Africa, 1941–1944', *Intelligence and National Security*, 11, no. 4 (October 1996), pp. 696–721.

Gaelle and Jean-Pierre Montfort *La Vie adventureuse du Breton Jean Bouguennec.*

Nouzille, Vincent, *L'Espionne: Virginia Hall, une Américaine dans la guerre.* Paris: Fayard, 2007.

O'Connor, Bernard, *RAF Tempsford Airfield: Churchill's Most Secret Airfield.* Stroud: Amberley Publishing, 2010 [Supersedes previous publications by the author on the same topic].

Pierre-Bloch, Jean, *Mes jours heureux.* Paris: Le Bateau Ivre, 1946.

Plas, Pascal (ed.), *Visages de la Résistance – 1940-1944: Libération de Limoges.* La Geneytouse: Éditions Lucien Souny, 2005.

Richards, Francis Brooks, *Secret Flotillas: The Clandestine Sea Lanes to France and French North Africa 1940-1944,* 2 vols (Government Official History), vol. 1 (*Clandestine Sea Lanes to France*), vol. 2 (*Clandestine Naval Operations 1940–1944*) (London: HMSO, 1996) [A second edition, with the titles altered slightly, appeared with Routledge in 2004].

Ross, Bernie, *Training SOE Saboteurs in World War Two* (web-site). Last updated 17 February 2011; accessed 31 July 2011 [Includes a very good bibliography].

Rousselier, Danièle, *Le colonel Rivier est mort.* Paris: Éditions Seuil, 1989.

Seaux, Dominique, 'Histoire: Il y a 65 ans: La bataille d'Egletons' [with photos], in: *La Lettre de Saint-Yrieix-le-déjalat: Bulletin municipal,* no. 17 (July 2009), p. 14 [also available on-line at www.saint-yrieix-le-dejalat.fr].

Sebag-Montefiore, Hugh, *Dunkirk: Fight to the Last Man.* London: Penguiwn, 2007.

Sereau, Raymond, *La Libération de la Corse (1943).* Paris: J. Peyronnet et Cie, 1955.

Silvani, Paul, *Et la Corse fut libérée,* 1st edition. Ajaccio: La Marge, 1993, 2nd (completely revised) edition (nouvelle edition complétée et refondu). Ajaccio: Albiana, 2002.

Verity, Hugh, *We Landed by Moonlight: Secret RAF Landings in France 1940–11.* Shepperton: Ian Allan Ltd, 1978.

Verrier, Anthony, *Assassination in Algiers: Churchill Roosevelt, De Gaulle and the Murder of Admiral Darlan.* New York: W. W. Norton, 1990.

Vickers, Philip, *Das Reich: 2nd SS Panzer Division 'Das Reich': Drive to Normandy June 1944.* Barnesley: Pen & Sword, 1999.

West, Nigel [pseud. Rupert Allason], *Secret War: The Story of SOE, Britain's Wartime Sabotage Organisation.* London: Hodder & Stoughton, 1992.

–––, **[pseud. Rupert Allason] (ed.),** *The Guy Liddell Diaries,* 2 vols (London: 2004-2009), i (Frank Cass Publishers, 2004), ii (Routledge, 2009).

Wilkinson, Peter and **Bright-Astley, Joan,** *Gubbins and SOE.* Barnsley: Pen & Sword Military Books, 1993.

Dickerson, Bryan J., From Liberation to Confrontation: The U.S. Army and Czechoslovakia 1945 to 1948.

Long, Christopher A., Dr George Rodocanachi.

Perrin, Nigel, Denis Rake.

– – –, Phillippe Liewer.

Tillet, Pierre, Tentative of History of In/Exfiltrations into/from France during WWII from 1941–1945.

Ross, Bernie, Training SOE Saboteurs in World War Two.

ARCHIVAL REFERENCES:

National Archives (Kew):

HS3/64 (Massingham)

HS6/968 (Miranda Prison 1941/42)

HS6/219, pp. 219-21 (Special Planning)

HS7/20 (SAARF)

HS7/21 (SAARF)

HS7/170 (Corsican Campaign)

HS7/218, p. 1267 (24 July 1941)

HS8/435, pp. 1040-5 (SOE Training Section)

HS8/1031 (Specimens of False Documents)

HS9/87/2 (Georges Val Barbier's Personal File)

HS9/115/21 (Georges Bégué's Personal File)

HS9/166/1 (Jean and Gaby Pierre-Bloch's Personal File)

HS9/630/10 (Jacques de Guélis's Personal File [includes service records in French and English])

HS9/647/4 (Virginia Hall's Personal File)

HS9/780/5 (Paul Colonna d'Istria's Personal File)

HS9/923/4 (Phillippe Liewer's Personal File)

HS9/1362/2 (André Simon's Personal File)

WO117/1039 (War Diary of Shenley Military Hospital 1941-45)

WO167/985 (War Diary of 234th Field Coy, RE, 1940-45)

WO309/2054

Other Archives:

The Archivo Militar de Guadalajara.

The Archives, Felsted School, Essex.

The Barbier Family Papers.

Max Hyman's Family Papers.

The Archives, Manchester Grammar School.

The Windsor Archives.

University Records, University of Cardiff.

Pseudos or code names of Resistance leaders et al – many of them mentioned in the radio messages sent and received by TOSCAN and CRÉTOIS.

ADJACENT – Bisset

ALOOF – Marcel Lacouture

ARC – Jacques Chaban-Delmas

ADDITION –

ADIABATIQUE – Claude Gros

ANASTASIE – Jacques Dufour

ANTOINE – FTP Roger / Robert?? Lecherbonnier

ARC – Jacques Chaban-Delmas

ARISTIDE – Major Roger Landes

BARON – Gérard Hennebert

BARTHELEMY –

BOHEMIEN – Vladimir Dolgopoloff

BERGAMOTE – Mission sud Creuse (7man)

CESARI – Paulin Colonna d'Istria

BARON – Gérard Hennebert

CLOTHAIRE, PACO – Bob Maloubier

COMETE – Raymond Fassin

CORIOLAN – Franz Saar-Demichel

CRETOIS – James Edgar (Tillleul)

CURVILIGNE – Jean Gorodiche - organise medical services

DIASTIQUE – André Simon (Tilleul)

DIVINER – Daniel Turberville

DURET – Jean Craplet AS

DUDULE – Robert de Schrevel aka Roger de Saule.

ELLIPSE – Eugène Dechelette, Délégué Militaire Regional pf R5

ESPACE – Jacques Polak

ESQUIMAUX –Henri Devilliers

FACE –André Bernard

GEORGES Col. – Marius Guédin AS

GEORGES – W/T operator

HANNIBAL – Joseph Fertig FTP

HEMISPHERE – Cecil Vincent Davin

HERVÉ-PATRICK– René Vaujour AS Chef Corrèze

HAMISH – JEDBURGH Team (Robert Anstett (Alabama) René Schmitt (Louisiana) Lee
  Waters (Kansas)

HAMLET, STAUNTON – Philippe Lieuwer

HICCUP, HOQUET – Jean le Harivel 1918-2006 Also GEORGES 25

HUBERT – ? Lieut. Colonel Léonard Hounau (Corps Franc Tulle)

ISOTHERME – Guy Vivier DMR /6

LOUIS – Léon Lanot

MANOMETRE – Jacques de Guélis Tilleul

MARQUIS – Paul Rivière

MINIMUM – Louis Monguilan (Thomas-Tilleul)

MINISTRE – René Molinier

MOLECULE – Jacques Robert Rewer –chef Bergamote (7 man mission).

NESTOR – Digger - Jacques Poirier

PACHA – Henri Guillaume

PAPE – Pierre Rateau (Thalamy) also VEGA and SIRIUS

POLYGONE – Maurice Bourges-Maurioury

PYRAMIDE – Courson

RIVIER – Maurice Rousselier

SEVERI – Fred Scaramoni

RIVIÈRE –Louis Marcel Godefroy

SIRIUS –

SOMMET – René Brutus

THERMOMÈTRE – Mackenzie (Tilleul)

TOSCAN – Lannou W/T Tilleul

TRIANGLE – Charles Gaillard. (Adjoint de Polygone)

TRIDENT – Antoine Salle?

VAUDREUIL

VECTEUR – Frederick Cardozo

VENITIEN –Josiane Somers (épouse Gros)

VICTOR – Jack Beresford Hayes

VIRGILE – Jean Claude Guiet

Back row from the left: Bob Maloubier, Jean Lannou, Jean-Claud Guiet, Jacques de Guélis, André Simon, Jacques Dufour. Front row: Charles Gaumondie, Fernand Philibert, Comm. Thomas, Marcel Lacouture, Ian Mackenzie.

THE PLANNING OF TILLEUL Vincennes GR 28 P 3 58 SHD

Mission TILLEUL originally called TRAPPER

Cipher telegram from Massingham – delighted at Jacques decision, BCRAA will make available 2 W/T operators here incl Lannou. A suggestion to put mission in from there (Algiers)

3 May – Jacques DR/M.1 to D/R wants to start collecting equipment (indent – requisition. Official order). Wants authority for 4 people – ie. The French officer, a British Officer and 2 W/t operators.

4 May – Re André Simon. Would take him on with his eyes fully open to any short-comings. He knows him well. (They had escaped together over the Pyrenees)

6 May – Wants approval for 2 S-phones and one Eureka. Jacques then had leave in May. (Family letter)

25 May – Back from leave. Area- part of the Massif Central. Team so far includes Bisset, Lannou shortly to arrive from Algiers. The second W/T op. to be British and a member of the Royal corps of signals so will be compelled to remain at all times at a protected HQ. Lannou to work direct to Massingham.

27 May – Jacques – Confirmation Corporal J Edgar, Intelligence corps to be attached to mission.

30 May – Jacques has met Thomas and believes he can work v. harmoniously with him.
Re Edgar – Jacques wants him promoted to sergeant

2 June – Jacques re Simon regarding his financial arrangements.

4 June – Massingham Measurement for Lannou's civvies.

15 June – Jacques – Financing TRAPPER. Will require two million francs and a thousand dollars. Name of op changed to TILLEUL
Under the command of ELLIPSE, DMR R5 (military zone)

16 June – Jacques confirm and clarify - mission ready apart from permits, travel .

19 June – Permission requested for Captain EGA Bisset (Gen.List) to go to the field on a maquis mission (TILLEUL.) Captain Bisset has been briefing officer in F section from September 1943 for 8 months. No access to SIS docs or correspondence or involvement w mil. planning. Duties consisted of briefing agents in the organisation of resistance, life in the field, topography and method of reception of operations. No access to security docs in this HQ.

22 June – Agree Captain Bisset can proceed to the Field.

28 June – Jacques wants to indent 500,000 frs for Mackenzie's use.

1 July – RF to EMFFI authority for TILLEUL to be supplied with 2 containers food, 1 of comforts and 3 of Piats to accompany them when they leave for the field.

3 July – EMFFI to RF De Guelis in full agreement to ground POIRE – a SALESMAN ground. SALESMAN to receive TILLEUL, hand over all contacts in the Correze and withdraw to his area to the west of this Dept. Make arrangements direct with F section for mounting and dispatch of this mission from Thursday 6 July.

No food as area not in short supply. One container comforts, no Piats in first instance.

5 July – F/Ops to RF SALESMAN has changed ground for receptiom of TRAPPER (TILLEUL) New ground is STATIONER 127 (10 km SW Eymoutiers) or alternative STATIONER 108. This op to be laid out from Friday July 7th. Probably Liberators from Harrington.

6 July – Re supplies. TILLEUL will be landing outside its area So supplies will be limited and to make immediate arrangements for the rest to be in its own territory. The equipment for the TILLEUL op. to be held till asked for and consists of the whole original order for W/T equipment minus the Eureka set and of the foll. containers:

C12-C13-C9 and H.7F (Special stores) + 2 gallon jars of rum The remaining space reserved for SALESMAN.

22 July – Mix up over CRETOIS messages. F and RF sections got their wires crossed at some stage and while TOSCAN's messages were being handled by EMFFI and Col O'Hanlon told F/ops not to take any action on messages from TILLEUL. This explains why CRETOIS' messages went unanswered and why Leo Marks told him they were all thrown in the waste paper basket. It took until 2016/17 for James Edgar to have this explanation to the mystery!

MISSION TILLEUL (with thanks to Dominique Seaux)

July 7/8 – Operation STATIONER 137 2 Liberators leave Harrington Airfield piloted by Choper and Driscoll arriving in the early hours at le Clos, Haute Vienne with reception by SALESMAN (Maloubier Staunton etc.)

9th – Ian Mackenzie meets FTP officer in charge of medical services and hands him 100,00F. De Guélis and Thomas (aka Monguilan) meet AS chief of Chamberet (Corrèze)

11th (or 12th according to de Guélis) – Escorted by René Pin, de Guélis and Thomas meet Lanot Leon (LOUIS) at Lamazière-Basse.

12th – The above two meet HANNIBAL (Joseph Fertig FTP) and Ct Duret (AS)

The Neuvic region and the Marèges dam prospected

14th – Mackenzie leaves for the Corrèze and treats a wounded man en route in the East Haute Vienne. He joins the mission at Chadebech. .. TILLEUL had settled at Marcy but had to leave for Chadebech (Bonnefond) and established their HQ at the home of Justin Sauviat.

14–18 July – Landing grounds 1st Series north of the RN89: The co-ordinates for landing ground LOUP sent then also CHAMEAU, VACHE (Bonnefond, Péret Bel-Air) COCHON, LAPIN.

20–31 July – Mackenzie at Mauriac (Cantal) to treat 'Chef de l'Etat Major

2nd Series: Co-ordinates sent for VEAU (Marcillac). TAUREAU (St. Angel), ECUREUIL (St. Augustin) CHAT(Clergoux).

Thalamy – COCARDE was never used, in spite of a great deal of preparation and messages back and forth over the month of August.

Bisset instructs young maquis at Lamazière-Basse in use of arms and explosives and in the art of ambush.

Jacques at Argentat and meets at their HQ HERVÉ (Vaujour), GEORGES (Marius Guédin AS chief Basse Corrèze) NESTOR (Jacques Poirier) DIGGER.

Jacques meets RIVIER (Maurice Rousselier) CURVILIGNE (Jean Gorodiche) at Chadebech and TRIDENT (Antoine Salle) at Bonnefond.

Night of 30/31 July – Reception of 36 containers from 2 planes on 'VACHE'. Two further planes dropped containers 20km away. The containers received on 5 August.

Night of 31 July/1 August – Parachute reception at LAPIN – 4 planes.

1 August – Mackenzie takes medical supplies to the hospital at Prés-Longs (St. Yrieix le Déjalat)

3 August – Mackenzie rejoined by Dr. Ravaine and Jeanine Nussbaumer.

A German column arrives at Egleton and occupies the school (Ecole Nationale Professionelle_ENP)

4 August – Hospital moved to La Virolle (St Yrieix le Déjalat).

5 August – André Simon at Thalamy. 6-10 August Work on the ground with BARON to make it viable.

Jacques and Thomas meet POLYGONE, RIVIER, RIVIÈRE, ADELINE, DUPONT, COPEAU at Neuvic.

Night of 9/10 August – Weather prevents drop at 'CHAMEAU' .

10 August – Meeting in the evening at Thalamy – André Simon, de Guélis, Thomas, with CURVILIGNE, BARON, SÉCATEUR, waiting for a landing. No landing ever here.

The importance given to Thalamy in radio messages was because it was the only landing ground in the Haute Corrèze and is still in use.

The aerodrome served several times for Lysanders to land between August, 1942 and January 1943. In 1943 the Germans dug trenches across it to render it unusable.

Night of 10/11 August – Capt. Wauthier, 30 SAS and TEAM JAMES land at 'COCHON'. (6 planes) André Simon present at reception.

11 August – André Simon present at a meeting between the Jedburghs and HUBERT.

12 August – Mackenzie moves hospital into St Yrieix le Déjalat (Maison Taguet and School).

De Guélis and Thomas meet ANTOINE (Roger Lecherbonnier FTP) who wants to attack the school. That evening with his agreement de Guélis and Thomas with one of his men attempt to obtain a surrender from the Germans. Refused.

14 August – Mackenzie recruits local help because of the large number of wounded needing treatment.

James Edgar (CRÉTOIS) alone at the Hotel Beau-Site at Saint Pardoux la Croisille. *See note in papers to do with preparation.*

Bisset at Egletons encouraging the men during the siege fighting. Gives instruction. De Guélis also present during the siege.

16 August – De Guélis and Thomas meet ELLIPSE (Eugène Déchelette 1906–1973, DMR for R5) for the first time and receive his instructions.

17 August – De Guélis and Thomas go to Ussel with arms and munitions and arrive in the middle of the battle. They meet DURET and DUDEUX who inform them of the arrival of the column (German) from Clermont. De Guélis visits Mackenzie at St. Yrieux on his return.

TILLEUL asks for the RAF to bomb the German column reported at Laqueuille (Puy de Dôme)

Night of the 17/18 August – Drop at 'LOUP' by 4 planes .

18 August – ESPACE(Jacques Polak) arrived and delivers a package to Mackenzie.

Tilleul insisting on an RAF attack on the German column.

19 August – Due to the German presence, Mackenzie sends some of his wounded to the hospital at Brigoux and others to the schoolhouse at Sarran.

Demand for RAF intervention repeated.

20 August – André Simon looking for another landing ground. TILLEUL asking for RAF action on the 22nd towards Eygurande.

The Corrèze liberated on the 22 August and on 26 August the Mission moves its HQ to Sainte Fortunade.

30 August – The mission meets ELLIPSE at Limoges, who asks them to stay in the Corrèze to help prevent abuses of power by certain individuals.

3 September – TEAM JAMES and the SAS group leave for La Creuse.

4 September – André Simon decides to renovate the aerodrome at Brive.

9 September – Both Simon and de Guélis and Major Staunton at Limoges for the arrival of MISSION GERMINAL (*OSS mission to contact all American operatives in SW France*) and Lieutenant Anstett (HAMISH) by Hudson bomber from Tempsford (*Major Staunton returned to London on the Hudson bomber with 8 stranded allied airmen and three others with secret orders*). There were no radio transmissions for two days.

10 September – The mission again at Sainte-Fortunade.

11 September – Mackenzie leaves the Corrèze for Limoges. Has to retrieve his medical supplies parachuted near Guéret from BERGAMOTE, another inter-allied seven-man mission dropped in the Creuse, head of mission, Jacques Robert-Rewez (MOLECULE).

14 September – Mackenzie leaves Limoges with Joly's column, James Edgar, Bisset and Thomas stay in the Limousin. While Simon and de Guélis leave in search of parachute grounds (Dijon, La Rochelle region, Bordeaux) Lannou leaves either with Joly or de Guélis

17 September – Edgar and Bisset decorated by Colonel Rivier. Thomas also in Limoges. Thomas returned to England on the 20 September

Edgar return to England on 23 September by Hudson from Le Blanc (Indre)

 Bisset left Limoges for Paris with Captain Fraser by car.

Vichy – 24 September – Bisset accidentally shot in front of the Hotel des Ambassadeurs. Both Simon and de Guélis return to Vichy due to Bisset's death and miss the decorations ceremony at Limoges.

24 September – Mackenzie arrives in Vichy to arrange Bisset's funeral.

25 September – (Germinal report) *At 09.30 hours, FFI guard of honour was formed outside the Hotel Radio, Allied Forces Officers who acted as honorary pall bearers were:*

Captian Grell, Captain Schley, Lt. Griffith, Lt. Cutting, Major Mackenzie, Captain Meuier, Captain Fraser and Sgt. Potter.

At 10.15 hours the body was taken to the Protestant Chapel where a brief service was held. The coffin was beautiful, covered with Union Jack and surrounded by wreaths presented by various units of the Allied Forces. The funeral procession was carried out in a military manner with a Guard of Honour formed by the FF1.

26 September. Captain Bisset was buried at 10.00 hours. The following American and British Officer were present:

Major Mackenzie, Major de Guellis (sic) Captain André Simon, Captain Grell, Captain Schley, Lt. Griffiths, Lt. Cutting and Sgt Potter.

The FFI again furnished a Guard of Honour, The body was interred in the Cimetière de Vichy.

5 October – Mackenzie back in London. Simon and de Guélis go to Paris. Meet Buckmaster at Hotel Cecil and Koenig at Les Invalides

8 October – In Paris De Guélis meets for the last time, his cousin Capt. GV Barbier (Val) who came with the troops from the south. They drank champagne together. Was back in London on 10 October and his cousin also returned to London in October

8 October – Thomas parachuted in the Pornic-Paimboef region to reinforce Mission Shinoile (secteur St.Nazaire).

Copy of a report from the 39th Evacuation Hospital, Weiden (HS7/20)

27th May 1943

To whom it may concern

This is to certify that Major J de Guelis has been under medical care for injuries sustained by him on the 16th May 1945.

Said injuries consisted of four fractured ribs, (Lt Maynard said eight in his report) contused wound of right kidney and multiple contusions of lower back and buttocks. This was complicated by a partial atelectasis and pneumonic process on opposite sides of the chest.

Evacuation will take place on the 28th June thru regular channels.

39 Evac.Hosp.

Copy of the Accident Report (HS7/20) – *See page 151*

By Lt.FG Maynard AAC
302835

On the 16th May at about 16.30 hrs I was driving a captured German vehicle along the road from Flossenburg to Weiden on duty. I was driving along a main road at approximately 35mph rounding a right curve; Suddenly a small camouflaged German car appeared out of a concealed side turning, about 20 yds in front of me. The car was driven by a German civilian working for the Concentration Camp at Flossenburg, named Dietrich. I applied my brakes and swerved to avoid the vehicle. But the driver took his hands off the wheel, started screaming and accelerated. The car was struck on the side door and my car somersaulted and turned over, we were all thrown clear of the car. Major de Guelis must have been injured on impact. I sent Sgt. Nicolls for an ambulance which arrived and took the Major to the 39th Evacuation Hospital.

Casualties: Major: 8 broken ribs, split liver, split kidneys.
                Lieut.: None
                Sgt: Thumb of right hand fractured.

Sgt Nicoll added something of interest in his report: that he was treated first at Flossenburg Camp Hospital and later at 39 US Evac.

Permissions

BB	Thanks to Bruno Barthelot for many photos
CA	Wrekin College Archives, thanks to archivist Mervyn Joiner
CBM	With permission of the Carpet Baggers Museum
CdeN	Thanks to the de Neuville family
DH	With thanks to Daniel Hymans
DS1	Thanks to Duncan Stuart
DS2	Thanks and permission to share to Dominique Seaux
F	Thanks to the family of Jean Bouguennec for book and permission to use a photo
GC	Georgette Chabrerie kindly agreed to my use of this photo
GI	Thanks to Gerald Isaaman
JC	Thank you to Andrew Croft's daughter Julia Corner for showing me her father's papers and for permission to use his photo
JE	Thanks to James Edgar for various photos including his portrait
JW	Thank you to Jon Wilson for photos and lots of help
PC	Photo Pierre Compiègne. Copy in author's possession
Po l	Permission on-line
SHD	Service Historique de la Défence, Vincennes
SW	Grateful thanks to Simon Worral who delivered photos of his father in person
TNA	The National Archives of the UK – WO107/985 and HS7/20
Wiki	By Eric Gaba (Sting – fr:Sting) for original blank map, Rama for zones – Own work
WB	The late Mrs Win Bisset

Source of data: NGDC World Data Bank II (public domain)
Image: France map Lambert-93 with regions and departments-blank.svg
GFDL
(Original link https://commons.wikimedia.org/w/index.php?curid=5285193)

ND - #0337 - 270225 - C0 - 234/170/11 - PB - 9781911604440 - Gloss Lamination